DISCOVER

- ▶ The real reasons that the record business is in such trouble today

- ▶ Legitimate alternatives to downloading music from pirate music services

- ▶ Cool ways to find new music and connect with your favorite artists

- ▶ How kids are changing the face of music marketing

- ▶ How the record industry gets into your head to make you buy music

- ▶ How video games have more influence in music than radio stations

- ▶ How you can benefit from the explosion in digital music

- ▶ The Top-10 Truths about the music industry that you may not know about

- ▶ What music has to learn from cable television

- ▶ How technology will completely rewire the music business

"*A fascinating read that takes the recent turmoil in the music business and gives it shape and form. Will help readers understand how the times have changed and some new ways of thinking about how to make it work for any number of people working in the music biz in the future.*"

—Charles McEnerney, Producer, Well Rounded Radio

"*Amid all the shouting and confusion, along comes* The Future of Music, *which in a calm and clear voice explains the essential issues roiling the music business today. Most importantly, this is written directly for musicians and their fans, rather than business people in the music industry. If you want to know what you're getting into as you develop your music career, and where music will be coming from in the future, you have to read this book.*"

—Gary Burton, Grammy-winning vibraphonist

"*Adapt or Perish:* The Future of Music *should be required reading for anyone hoping to make a living in any profession even peripherally affected by the entertainment industry.*"

—James Harrington, The Groove

"The Future of Music *offers an enticing and provocative vision for the future of an industry in dire need of reinvention. For newcomers and industry veterans alike, Kusek and Leonhard paint a picture of tomorrow's music business that is at once dynamic, challenging, ever changing, and unlimited in its potential. What else would we wish the future to be?*"

—Eric Beall, VP, Sony/ATV Music

"*Some may find this book controversial while others will consider it prophesy. Kusek and Leonhard have managed to tap into the problems—and possibly the solutions—of an industry at the crossroads. For those of us who left the record business to go into the music business, video games are the new rock 'n' roll. But no matter where this revolution begins or ends, the industry must learn to respect and react to its consumers. This book contains valuable insights for us all.*"

—Steve Schnur, Worldwide Executive of Music, Electronic Arts

"Kusek and Leonhard lay out critical visions of the past, present, and future. A must-read for music and media culture futurists."

—Mike Dreese, CEO, Newbury Comics

"As a veteran of the wars between the mighty music publishing conglomerates and those rare individuals who still cherish 'intellectual property rights,' I read The Future of Music *with great interest. Kusek and Leonhard have done an engaging job of presenting some imaginative yet realistic alternatives for an ever-changing industry. Deep down I hope they are wrong, but I doubt it."*

—Steve Karmen, composer of "I Love New York," author of *Who Killed the Jingle?*

"If you are a musician looking to better reach your audience, or a musical entrepreneur hoping to succeed in the music industry, this book is for you! Technology advances in the last ten years have transformed the music business, and The Future of Music *takes a fresh look at the major issues facing artists, music consumers, and the recording industry, and provides truly creative insights into the next wave of the music business."*

—David Mash, VP for Information Technology, Berklee College of Music

"In The Future of Music, *Kusek and Leonhard take their place among the visionaries of this fascinating industry. In this thought-provoking and informative book, they take the reader on a journey to the rich future that music and technology may bring us if we heed their warnings about wise choices that must be made today. "*

—Joel Fisch, Senior Investment Manager, Intel Capital

"A stunningly candid source of concentrated, up-to-date insight about the music business and its turbulent transition into the digital era. I've dreamed about a book like this...I can't think of any book more important for artists to get the full re-orientation they need to survive and prosper in the digital era. It's no less critical for members of the music and broadcasting industries who need to consolidate their thinking into a coherent roadmap for the future. In a word: indispensable."

—Stephen Hill, Producer, Hearts of Space

THE FUTURE OF MUSIC

MANIFESTO FOR THE DIGITAL MUSIC REVOLUTION

DAVID KUSEK

GERD LEONHARD

Edited by Susan Gedutis Lindsay

Berklee Media

Vice President: David Kusek
Dean of Continuing Education: Debbie Cavalier
Director of Business Affairs: Robert Green
Associate Director of Technology: Mike Serio
Marketing Manager, Berkleemusic: Barry Kelly
Senior Graphic Designer: David Ehlers

Berklee Press

Senior Writer/Editor: Jonathan Feist
Senior Writer/Editor: Susan Gedutis Lindsay
Production Manager: Shawn Girsberger
Marketing Manager, Berklee Press: Jennifer D'Angora
Product Marketing Manager: David Goldberg

Printed in the United States of America.

12 11 10 09 08 07 06 05   6 5 4 3 2 1

Library of Congress Cataloging-in-Publication Data
Kusek, David, 1955-
  The future of music / David Kusek, Leonhard Gerd.
      p. cm.
  Includes index.
  ISBN-13: 978-0-87639-059-7
  ISBN-10: 0-87639-059-9
  1. Music trade. 2. Sound recording industry. I. Leonhard, Gerd, 1961- II. Title.
  ML3790.K86 2005
  381'.4578'0266–dc22
                                        2004025942

1140 Boylston Street
Boston, MA 02215-3693 USA
(617) 747-2146
Visit Berklee Press Online at
www.berkleepress.com

DISTRIBUTED BY

HAL•LEONARD®
CORPORATION
7777 W. BLUEMOUND RD. P.O. BOX 13819
MILWAUKEE, WISCONSIN 53213

Visit Hal Leonard Online at
www.halleonard.com

Contents

Acknowledgments

Many thanks to Berklee researchers Laura Burczak, Eric Schleicher, Ariane Martins, Margie Braunstein, and Doug Hampton-Dowson for helping to gather the data and stories used in this book. Don Gorder, Chair of the Music Business Department at Berklee College of Music, and Berklee Professor Peter Alhadeff provided invaluable help and advice. Jim Griffin, John Parres, and all the members of the PhoList sparked our minds and fueled our discussions countless times, and to the Electronic Frontier Foundation: Keep up the good work. Thanks also to John Perry Barlow, for your inspiration and encouraging talks, and Lawrence Lessig and the Creative Commons for providing a pointer towards the future. And finally, thank you to our editor Susan Gedutis Lindsay for helping us put this book together and blending our thoughts into a single voice.

This book, Berklee College of Music, and the authors have no association with the Future of Music Coalition.

Introduction

This is a book about music and the music business in the twenty-first century. Imagine a world where music flows all around us, like water, or like electricity, and where access to music becomes a kind of "utility." Not for free, per se, but certainly for what feels like free.

In this world, we share, contribute, collaborate, and trade music amid a constant flow of new songs that suit our tastes and preferences, without any palpable constraints or limitations. Music is ubiquitous and served up in easy, friendly formats. Like water (at least in the developed parts of the world), it is simply present just about everywhere, anytime.

Artists, writers, composers, and producers all prosper, both creatively and financially. The music industry is redefined from A to Z, as fairer, bigger, and better. Fans, artists, and all kinds of music communities *drive* the business, rather than *being driven* by corporate powers. Sound interesting? Read on.

Ever since the invention of electricity, music and technology have worked hand-in-hand, and technology continues to catapult music to unprecedented heights. Today, because of the Internet and other digital networks, and despite all the legal wrangling, *music is bigger* than ever before. Within ten to fifteen years, the "Music Like Water" business model that we will outline in this book will make the industry two or three times larger than it is today.

Right now, the music industry is viewed as being in great turmoil. Technology has brought powerful and disruptive changes to the ruling incumbents. The best-selling CD in the U.S. is a blank, recordable one. Profits at the big record labels have dwindled and the markets for recorded music have virtually collapsed in many other parts of the world.

Will record companies go the way of horse-drawn carts? How will music companies make money in the future? Who will buy—that is, pay for—music, for how much, and on what terms? How do music fans feel about these developments, and how will the artists deal with this? How is it all going to shake out? Is the music industry just the first of the so-called "creative industries" to be sold out for free via the digital networks, or will everyone be better off in a world of ubiqui-tous media? Whose views will prove to be more correct: the recording industry's legal sharks or burn-crazy downloading teenagers?

This book will examine the issues important to the future of music. We will uncover opportunities, plunge into challenges, serve up wildcards, and revel in utopia. We will move from mere facts through dazzling stories to far-out visions and fantasies. Our views, along with those of other artists, writers, and industry insiders, attempt to give some insight into what is really happening, and what it will mean for the people who love music and for the people who make music.

We see ourselves not as predicting the future by any scientific means, but as providing inspiration, in order to jumpstart your imag-ination and get you juiced up about the future of music. A brave new world is waiting for those who can handle it—a world that very likely holds fantastic business opportunities for creative thinkers. Enjoy!

Music Like Water

It's the year 2015 and you wake to a familiar tune playing softly. It gets you out of bed and makes you feel good. As you walk into the bathroom, your Personal Media Minder activates the video display in the mirror, and you watch a bit of personalized news while you get ready for the day. You step into the shower and your personalized music program is ready for you, cued up with a new live version of a track that you downloaded the other day. It is even better than the original recording, so while you dress, you tell your "Taste-Mate" program to include the new track in your playlist rotation.

You put on your new eyeglasses, which contain a networked audio headset, letting tiny earbuds slip into your ears. You switch on the power, and the mix that your friend made for you starts to play. Music pours into your consciousness. It becomes yours.

After breakfast with the family, you head off to work and the Personal Media Minder asks if you wish to finish the audio book you started yesterday morning. You confirm and listen while you walk to the train that takes you to your job.

During the day, your headset and other wireless devices help you communicate across the network, with your friends, associates, network buddies, and "digital peers." The headset also keeps you connected to that hard rock collection that you really love to listen to. Meanwhile, a variety of new songs, new versions, and remixes of tracks you truly dig, along with your old favorites, continues to come your way. Using TasteMate, you access and trade playlists, and recommend a couple of songs to your friend in Seattle, and they get added to his rotation. Music propels you throughout the day.

On the way home, you choose your usual dose of news, sports, weather, and the latest dirt on your favorite bands and movie stars. The headset syncs to the active 3D displays that project images just in front of your eyes, or onto the communal screens available on the train and at home. You decide what you hear and see, and who can share in the experience. The Media Minder blends and delivers the programming you select, along with whatever variety of new music you decide to explore. It also determines how that new music is chosen, with the help of the TasteMate program.

Back at home, you cruise into the evening with the house system sending soft dinner jazz to various speaker systems in your house, as you serve up one of your culinary specialties, then pay your bills. One of these bills is your media and entertainment subscription, which includes your monthly music, video, network, and communications charges; it's always lower than your heating or water bill. Incoming calls from your friends blend into the programming that surrounds you, as you see fit. After dinner, you clean up, perhaps enjoy a couple of games with friends across your virtual network, and begin to wind down with some New-Age derivatives of Mozart's original compositions, which you discovered late one night while cruising through the music sharing channels. . . .

This, we believe, is a possible scenario from the future of music—a future in which music will be like water: ubiquitous and free flowing. Our views are not definitive, precise, or all-inclusive, but simply are snapshots of the future. In this future, music will be ubiquitous, mobile, shareable, and as pervasive and diverse as the human cultures that create it. Many of the already ill-fitting definitions of copyright and intellectual property and patent laws will be adapted to fit the "music like water" model that we propose—in a way that ensures the enjoyment and benefit of society as a whole, and that allows all involved parties to prosper.

David Bowie encapsulated the current state of affairs in a June 2002 *New York Times* article:

> The absolute transformation of everything that we ever thought about music will take place within ten years, and nothing is going to be able to stop it. I see absolutely no point in pretending that it's not going to happen. I'm fully confident that copyright, for instance, will no longer exist in ten years, and authorship and intellectual property is in for such a bashing. Music itself is going to become like running water or electricity. [. . .] So it's like, just take advantage of these last few years because none of this is ever going to happen again. You'd better be prepared for doing a lot of touring because that's really the only unique situation that's going to be left. It's terribly exciting. But on the other hand it doesn't matter if you think it's exciting or not; it's what's going to happen . . .

A Digital Music Primer

Beginning with the introduction of the compact disc (CD) into the marketplace in the early 1980s, the music industry began a transformation from analog to digital—a change that has precipitated the transformation of music as a product into music as an entertainment service. By digitizing music and distributing it on the CD, the music industry made it possible for just about anyone to make an infinite number of perfect digital copies of every song ever released on CD. In so doing, the industry opened itself up to the massive changes we're seeing today.

The decision to adopt the digital CD format set the stage for the current debates and struggles, as well as the ongoing litigation over copyright and the ownership and control of music—ultimately leading to the far-reaching question of whether access will replace ownership. After all, if you can hear whatever you like, whenever you want to hear it, then you don't have to "own" or physically possess the music.

The CD is a wholly unprotected digital format, traditionally without any Digital Rights Management (DRM) or copy-protection mechanisms that prevent copies from being made. In the early 1990s, personal computer companies such as Dell, Gateway, Compaq, Hewlett-Packard, and Apple saw the potential of audio applications, and began to develop affordable consumer machines that included CD-ROM devices. Soon thereafter, high-quality speakers became an integral part of the personal computer, often bundled or built into the computer itself. The combination of CD-ROM and DVD-ROM drives, software, and Internet connections made it possible for consumers to "rip" music off their CDs and trade digital MP3 files via the World Wide Web, instant messaging, and e-mail.

MP3 is shorthand for a software algorithm that was developed to compress audio and video files for easier use in multimedia applications. This compression/decompression algorithm, or codec, is part of an international standard known as ISO-MPEG Audio Layer-3, pioneered by the German Frauenhofer Institute. The codec converts the data it into an MP3 file (with a 1:10 compression)—in a matter of seconds, on a personal computer. The combination of the CD format, personal computers, and the Internet was a true convergence of technologies that, in combination, started to tear the very heart out of the control that the music industry had over its product.

It was only a matter of time before college students began posting large collections of MP3s on college servers and Internet Web sites, where the songs could be downloaded by anyone. The proliferation and spread of MP3 files online, plus the difficulty one has in finding a particular file, caught the attention of Northeastern University student Shawn Fanning. Driven to create a simple way to organize and find MP3 files online, Fanning created Napster, a software application that quickly became one of the most well-known and widely publicized programs in history.

Napster was the first in a series of peer-to-peer systems, through which people could share and swap their files by remotely accessing each other's hard drives, rather than accessing a central server. The decentralized nature of peer-to-peer (P2P) applications enabled massive numbers of files to be accessed simultaneously by literally millions of users at one time.

The major record companies—namely Universal, Sony BMG, Warner, and EMI—felt so threatened by Napster and its progeny that they joined forces to sue Napster out of business. Led by the Recording Industry Association of America (RIAA) and its then-CEO Hilary Rosen, they waged war on companies, individuals, and technologies that they perceived were enabling the widespread piracy of their property, protected by copyright law and propelled by the Digital Millennium Copyright Act (DMCA).

The publicity surrounding the legal battles was extraordinary, but its result was not exactly what the labels had hoped for. The labels were so vigorous in their pursuit of "evil" Napster music pirates that they appeared to have pushed their own customers into an unstoppable feeding frenzy for online music. Napster filed for bankruptcy protection in 2002, but software developers around the world have been creating P2P applications to fill the vacuum it left, and the online sharing of MP3 files has continued unabated.

Using approaches similar to Napster, but technically and legally more insidious and clever, companies and P2P file-sharing systems including Kazaa, Morpheus, Grokster, iMesh, and Limewire have grown stronger than Napster ever was. It is estimated that hundreds of millions of copies of these free software applications have been downloaded, and that millions of people are online trading music files every minute of every day around the world. No wonder the record labels are worried.

In 2003, a legitimate yet tentative digital music market began to take hold. Steve Jobs and his team at Apple Computer convinced all five major record companies to license their songs to Apple for distribution via the new iTunes music store. That effort, reinforced by Apple's enormous "Rip, Mix, Burn" digital music marketing campaign, was a breakthrough for a legitimate online digital music market.

Despite Apple's efforts, it may prove impossible to compete with "free." The P2P onslaught may indeed destroy the current record companies, but that is not preventing the existing copyright holders from trying to keep control. The lack of cooperation and compromise in enabling new business models to be tested has actually encouraged file-sharing and the systems that support it. The future may be uncertain, but the present is known: the existence of such widespread file-sharing systems is a direct result of the incumbents failing to come to terms with the new digital reality.

Music Today

Contrary to what we've been hearing for the past three years, the *music business* is still in very good shape today. The problem is with the *record industry* and CD sales. The Big-4 major label groups, Sony BMG, Universal Music Group, EMI, and Warner, are all suffering. But if one looks beyond CD sales, it is clear that, *overall,* the music market is vibrant and alive. More music has been enjoyed over the past two or three years than ever before, by a factor of two or more. Music fans can thank the inventors and purveyors of new technologies—in particular, file-sharing services such as the original Napster and Kazaa. They also owe their good fortune to consumer electronics companies, the creators of computer games, DVDs, cell phone ring tones, and CD technologies that allow users to rip and burn their own CDs on personal computers. Music fans are completely awash in music, and digital music has become the new radio for the Internet generation. Digital technologies have been totally and unobtrusively integrated into the lifestyle of new generations of teens and young adults.

Access to music has never been easier, and music is thriving on both a regional and global level. Rock, singer/songwriter, bluegrass, hip-hop, heavy metal, DJ versions and remixes, and ethnic music of every variety, including Brazilian, Cuban, and African, are just some of the types of music enjoying tremendous success today. The Internet, and digital networks in general, are starting to flip the niche genres from the bottom to the top.

Despite a severe downturn in CD sales over the past four years, the U.S. concert business is soaring, rising four years straight, from $1.3 billion in 1998 to $2.1 billion in 2003, according to *Pollstar* magazine. Live music is bigger than ever, even with the recent summer slump in U.S. concert ticket sales.

However, things are going to get a lot worse for the record companies and for music stores and CD retailers, in particular. As of 2003, overall "record" (CD) sales were down 26 percent from their peak in 2000, and the total revenue is down some $2 billion. During this period, over twelve hundred U.S. music retailers have closed their doors, and many more are predicted to follow. The reason for the sorry state of record retailing has more to do with the behavior of the record companies themselves than with the impact of digital music and its users. In the 1990s, the labels shifted their primary distribution channel away from the traditional record store and over to the "big box" retailers such as Best Buy, Target, and Wal-Mart, all of which sell CDs at heavily discounted prices in order to attract crowds into their stores. This retail shift has been going on for the past ten years for most consumer goods. It has sharply reduced the amount of square footage available to record companies for presenting their wares, and ultimately reduced the variety of titles available to fans in stores.

The music business is going through a massively disruptive sea change that shakes the very foundations of the long-serving cartels in the recorded music business. A textbook example of the traditional music-business operating mode is Colonel Tom Parker, Elvis Presley's manager. Colonel Parker in many ways may be considered the person-ification of the larger-than-life manager, and he profited from auda-ciously exploiting Elvis. "The Colonel" set the pace for a lot of people who came after him, both in the record business as well as in the management business. While the "Colonel Parker" mode of operation seemed to have worked well for a long time—at least for some of the parties—this model now clearly has been outmoded by technology.

Technology is bringing about massive industry discontinuities, just as it did in the film industry when television was born. Movie theaters initially regarded television as a major threat. Likewise, when radio was born, music publishers went to court to try to shut down the first radio stations. When industries are forced to face extremely painful and sometimes counterintuitive changes, established companies often whither away, leaving room for more agile entrepreneurs. Witness what Bill Gates and Microsoft did to Digital Equipment Corp., Wang Laboratories, Honeywell, and IBM.

With any major industry transition, the most successful businesses do not waste time negating the new; rather, they figure out how to embrace it before being outmoded by it. You don't want to be the ice man still trying to deliver blocks of ice when everyone has a freezer of his or her own.

So why is the music industry, by and large, still fighting the digital "music like water" vision, tooth and nail? Because the industry's "leaders" are caught up in a storm of opposing ideologies: on the one side, the elusive and certainly terrifying anarchy of free information on digital networks, and on the other, their obsession with control of the media oligopolies. They are stuck in the middle, without enough wiggle room to make a move. Music publishing rights are among the most difficult to negotiate for because the market is controlled geographically, and securing the global rights for music is almost impossible to achieve.

Rather than anticipating and exploiting trends—which is what the music business *used to be* good at—the industry has moved to try to derail them, and to squash opportunities that change the way things are done. Before too long, however, it will be abundantly clear that trying to sell overpriced plastic discs to people who have ubiquitous online access to the entire vault of music will be like trying to sell snow at the North Pole.

The Ubiquity of Water

Water plays a very essential role in our lives—nothing happens without water. Hundreds of thousands of people around the globe work on supplying water to everyone else, billions are spent on ensuring a steady water supply, and armies of researchers and workers deal with water-related projects. Along with air, water is an absolute essential of life. We do not pay for air—yet—but we do pay for water, and consequently some water utility companies are among the richest companies on the planet.

Despite the huge economic significance of water, and the clout that these "utility" companies have, how do we pay for it? Do we feel that water companies have undue monopolistic powers, and do we consider water to be a "product?" We more or less voluntarily pay for water, yes, but we hardly notice it anymore; the expense has become a fact of life. The payments are woven into the fabric of nearly everyone's monetary routines; no individual fees are charged if you shower at the gym, if you wash your hands in a public restroom, if you use a drinking fountain, or if you fill up your car radiator.

Interestingly enough, despite the ubiquity of water in most of the developed world, there is a vast market for "premium water"— bottled drinking water that appears to be better or different than tap water. Today, people may pay more for a bottle of Pellegrino or Evian than for a pint of Budweiser or even a gallon of gasoline! They pay for the ability to get "special" water that it is guaranteed to be free of bacteria, for the packaging that makes it convenient to carry, for the refrigeration that keeps it cool, and, in some cases, for added carbonation or flavoring.

Could this model apply to the music business? Can we conceive of some kind of public utility model for music that would make any and all music available on a flat-fee basis, or on a very low "by-the-gallon" fee schedule? Could music be acceptable as a part of the cost of living, a nominal expenditure that we plan for?

It wasn't too long ago that a leading water company, France's Society General de L'Eau, morphed into a global media and entertainment company (Vivendi-Universal), and tried to dominate the music space. Its CEO at the time, the now-infamous Jean-Marie Messier, embarked on a mission that was based on a very similar "content utility" concept. His approach may now seem financially risky and badly timed, but the future may at least partially vindicate it.

If we zoom back to the days before water was ubiquitously available (and ubiquitously paid for), some people *did* have to pay right then and there to obtain their water, on a case-by-case basis. Fights broke out over access to water, and in Africa and the Middle East, many wars were fought over access to water. In the Europe of the Middle Ages, access to water was often subject to complex negotiations and fee payments. When piping and plumbing became so omnipresent that almost everyone could simply turn on a faucet and, voilá, the water would flow freely and magically, the entire pricing system changed very quickly into a *public utility* structure. New companies and service providers emerged, and the user benefited. Is this same process now beginning to take shape in the music business?

Utilities

Let's take a look at a utility model in the broadcast television industry. In some European countries, such as Germany and Austria, all residents that have televisions or radios in their homes, regardless of how or whether they use them, must pay a yearly flat fee to the government. The government then uses the funds to pay for public television and radio productions. This model, which resembles the "media like water" concept, is by and large accepted by millions of people. People pay an average of $100–150 per year in return for what feels like a free, unlimited, and unmonitored supply of media programming.

In contrast, the U.S. system of television broadcasting relies entirely on advertising revenues. This system certainly has its own merits and encumbrances, but, like the European system, it creates what music futurist Jim Griffin of Cherry Lane Digital calls a "pool of money" that pays for the production and the dissemination of television programs. The basic trade of "you watch the ads and we will give you the programs for free" also offers an interesting contribution for our "music like water" mantra: could it be that, a few years down the road, I will be able listen to music on a digital network if I also accept some advertising? Or, will I be able to pay a fairly low yearly fee for all-I-can-eat access on digital networks, and subject myself to some targeted advertising to get additional access to some premium content? Cable television in Europe has shown the way here, as well. Most residents pay both for the public broadcasts and for their cable television providers—and, they rent videos and DVDs, as well.

If we continue to riff on the idea of such a flat-fee utility model for music, the basic connectivity to the digital music network and that much-talked-about "celestial jukebox" would be next to free. In fact, the network may be bundled with other media utilities as in our example above, and thus be cost-neutral. We would be able to enjoy the basic music service for very little out-of-pocket cash. It would feel free to us, but would still generate significant revenue in the aggregate. That is the value of a large network; individuals each pay very little, but as an aggregate, they create a large pool of money.

Keep in mind that in most places around the globe, there are relatively few restrictions on when and how we use water. If we decided to fill our swimming pools with fresh water on a daily basis, nobody would give us a hard time . . . except during a drought . . . though our water bill would be proportionally larger, for sure. But still: no policing, no restrictions, no real-time control, and most importantly, no hassles. We pay little for the basics, and accept higher payments for added values. No water "rights management," no additional payment points, no jumping through hoops.

How would this work for the music business? How will we offer a basic music service that flows freely, anywhere, anytime? Until now, music was only sold in "Pellegrino" bottles, but customers are starting to discover the unstoppable "tap water" music that seems to be flowing freely on the 'Net. Yes, the quality is not the same, and it's not entirely legal (to say the least), but the benefits to the users still outweigh the drawbacks. There are certainly differences between CD-quality sound and MP3 digital music formats, but the difference is insignificant if "pricing" is considered.

Just imagine how much it would cost you to fill up your bathtub with gallons of Evian! Is it surprising that people are looking for an "online music faucet" rather than continuing to buy overpriced bottled music? Why not offer an even better "Evian" to people who may still want it, *and* utilize the existing technologies to supply the "tap water" music, too? Couldn't businesses make more money by supplying all the water, rather than just a limited fraction of it? Could companies thrive by providing ubiquitous access, rather than strong-arming the market by limiting the supply of music to drive up its value and thus create an artificial scarcity scenario?

In this book, we will attempt to outline the consequences of a future in which music is offered like water, with "music faucets" turned on, anywhere and anytime, and with large-scale users paying more to use more. Bottled water—i.e., new types of music products—will have a whole new life ahead of them, but this will no longer be the only way to get your music.

Music: A Product or Service?

Let's zoom back to 1887, when Emil Berliner invented the gramophone. Back then, the big deal was that the gramophone allowed people to listen to music *without having to actually be at the performance.* It forever changed the concept of music from a dynamic and interactive entertainment experience to a fixed product. Music became nearly synonymous with the medium that delivered it, beginning with wax cylinder, then vinyl disk, followed by cassette tape, and eventually, compact disc. In essence, music moved from being a performance and a service to being a product.

Because of this, we have become accustomed to the perfection and repeatable quality of today's music. Prior to the nineteenth century, music wasn't played the exact same way more than once, since it was impossible to reproduce the exact circumstances of a performance. The instruments and orchestration would change, as would the performers, their moods, audiences, and performance environments. Songs were performed as well as they could be in that moment, and composers worked hard to create a continuous flow of fresh music for fairs, operas, concerts, trade shows, theaters, and so forth. The composers of the time also liberally borrowed material from one another, often adapting, updating, and improving the songs for the players and performances at hand.

After more than a century of music being pitched and sold primarily as static products, with musicians getting paid to perform on such products, we are, in a way, returning to those early days, and music can once again become more about the experience than the product. Of course there are some styles of music that have never ceased to be a service, such as in niche markets, including classical music, world music, and jazz. Yet, most financially successful musicians have become purveyors of products, and hope to make a significant part of their living by "selling plastic."

Perhaps, as in the past, we can once again become part of the experience of music, rather than the static purchasers of it. We can be involved, we can cheer our favorite artists on, we can participate in events and react to them, and we can actually make a difference—as the audience or the creator, or both. This fits in nicely with a general trend in our society, of moving, step-by-step, from the "Information Society" via the "Knowledge Economy" to the "Experience Society," as we will explore in this book—that is, from a place where we are mere recipients of a flow of data and information, as in the traditional media models, to a place in which a lot more value is being placed on experiencing things first-hand and unfiltered.

Today, technology is empowering artists to communicate directly with their fans. The digital distribution of music will gradually minimize the pay-for-product mentality that has dominated the music business for over a century, and technology may finally create some deeper empowerment for more of the involved parties. This is bound to happen, despite the obviously Darwinian survival-of-the-fittest pressures that a more efficient system of interaction and commerce are also bound to produce; it will be even harder for new artists to get to any level of meaningful exposure when there are more artists trying to get attention in the various distribution channels.

However, empowerment of the consumer (much less the artist) is not what most record labels, AKA the purveyors of the product, have in mind. In fact, their lobbyists are fighting fiercely to prevent such things from happening. If music won't remain a product, then how could the labels possibly control access and pricing, get a straight line into your wallet, tell you what is available and what is not, or dictate what an artist will release and when and where? The thought that you and I, the consumers, will be *involved* in this process reads like blasphemy to a lot of the decision-makers in the music business. Their old-school system worked beautifully with Elvis, Janis Joplin, Jimi Hendrix, and the Backstreet Boys—a carefree club of willing co-dependents—but nevertheless, "the times, they are a-changing."

Now, powered by ever-mutating technology and the perpetually unquenchable desire of any artist to escape the dismal prison of obscurity, music is starting to flow into any and all digital networks, whether paid for or not, and whether authorized or not. As John Perry

Barlow, Grateful Dead lyricist and founder of the Electronic Frontier Foundation, reminds us, "Nature abhors a vacuum."

Further, digital networks are turning wireless faster than you can say, "You've got mail." "Mobile" will be more of a transformative activity than "online" ever was. Technologies that depend on cables and wires are slowly but surely fading into the past, because people tend to favor innovations that seamlessly integrate into their lives without obstacle. Human life is not hard-wired and is mostly spent on the move. This very basic aspect of humanity needs to be vigilantly considered when talking about the music business of the future: people are mobile, and increasingly so. They take all kinds of stuff with them and move around more than ever before. Clearly, the future of music belongs to truly mobile products and services: anything, anytime, anywhere.

The emerging "mobile" economy enables access to your music collections anytime and anywhere, in a beloved, heavenly, customized jukebox. The world's largest telecommunications companies, including AT&T, SBC, France Telecom, British Telecom, and Deutsche Telecom, are beginning to shift their strategies, placing an increasing emphasis on services and partnerships to enable the global distribution of content. Today, other companies are starting to develop the next generation of mobile music technologies. For example, Apple, Creative, Philips, Roku, Netgear, and others are developing networked media players that broadcast MP3 music from your computer wirelessly around your home or office. By 2005, nearly half of the thirteen thousand McDonald's restaurants in the U.S. will have WiFi installed, delivering music brought to you by Sony.

But this digital mobility does not really fit into the current value paradigms that have brought in the bacon for the music business. Ubiquitous digital mobility requires interoperability between devices in all territories, bulk-rate and subscription pricing, globally coordinated marketing activities, and a total redesign of music retailing and packaging. Therefore, the old ship may have to sink before the new one can launch.

There is no doubt that, due to the nature of people's music consumption habits, mobility is the major driver behind the latest developments. People like to listen to music everywhere—at home or on the road, while waiting, or while socializing. The total support of the mobility paradigm is what drove radio, in the early days, and that's what will drive digital music. Once wireless network access is an affordable and reliable standard around the world, digital music will take off and soar.

Let's look at the unprecedented options that a wireless device ultimately offers to the music fan: it can be always-on, and thus is constantly updateable and in tune with the user's peers and personal programming "agents," allowing for recommendations, discussions about music, and the easy sharing of interests, opinions, and of course, the music itself. Streaming music rather than downloading it will quickly become a viable option, once networks provide a truly acceptable sound quality and simplified pricing.

The increasing multitude of choices will outpace the single-minded purveyors of intellectual property that have sold us "culture" as a solid good for the past one hundred years. This process is as inevitable as the one that made people put their horses out to pasture and switch to cars and planes as a prime mode of transportation. Nobody would stick with horses just because some blacksmith fears a decline in horseshoe sales. People are simply exercising their right to choose. Having more options will lead to more diversity, more niche markets, and more opportunities for artists, writers, and music businesses.

More and more, the average consumer is following the course charted by the early adopters of new technologies—the "influencers"—who, as recent research reports have proven, are as wired-up and connected as one could imagine, and vastly prefer the Internet over any other medium. The gaming industry, for one, has already followed this call, and has come up with products that are easy to use, interactive, and give the consumer what they want, thereby driving revenues that make music industry executives green with envy.

When artists stop thinking of themselves as providers of solid goods, then the doors will open for a much wider variety of music to flood into limitless and low-friction distribution channels, without five or ten or even twenty companies gating the flow of content. Having said that, though, it will be more important than ever to creatively program and present all this new music in ways that make it easy, fun, and rewarding for consumers to find what they like.

Wild Card: The Universal Mobile Device (UMD)

June 1, 2015. Our Universal Mobile Devices (UMD) are "always-on" at 8 MB/second, and we have anytime-anywhere access to music, films, games, books, news, streaming video, online banking, stock market transactions, instant messaging, e-mail, and chats. It's a global telephone, a digital communication and data transfer device, a Global Positioning Device (GPS), a personal digital assistant, a music/images/film storage device, a recorder, a personal computer, a gaming platform . . . and much more that we haven't even gotten around to trying yet. Still, it is only a little bit larger than a cigarette pack, its processor is one hundred times as fast as the good old Intel Centrino chip, and with over 5 terabytes of data storage, there is plenty of room for anything we want. Our UMD can project a fairly large and sharp image onto any white surface, it can set up instant secure wireless connections to other computers, beamers, monitors, screens, and printers, and it can connect to other UMDs to exchange data and files, instantly and securely.

The UMD "off-road" version is so durable that you can drive a truck over it, or leave it out in the rain for a few days. Ten days of battery power lets us forget about hunting for electric outlets everywhere we go. In short, our UMDs are irresistible, and sometimes we even struggle with ourselves to put them away.

And how much do we pay to get this device and the wireless service? Less than what a year of dial-up Internet service used to cost only ten years ago. Speaking of those days, we are so relieved to have lost all the cables, the multiple billing procedures, the restrictions on usage, the endless calls to customer service to figure out how to make it work, the non-compatibility, and all of the other burdens. Now, the pricing—and what you get for your money—is so compelling that everyone considers it a part of their basic expenses, like the phone bill, cable television, or car registrations.

Today, the basic content service comes packaged with the monthly service fee, and a content levy is imposed on the device itself. It took ten years for the device makers, software providers, and entertainment companies to agree on a voluntary compulsory licensing scheme, but now the content providers make much more money than they did before UMDs were around. In addition, their marketing costs have shrunk to one tenth of what they used to be, their delivery costs keep falling, administration and accounting is handled by smart automated software agents, and their legal budgets have been reduced to a fraction of what they used to be because there is nothing left to sue for. Finding cool new stuff rules the day. Get our attention, and let us make a connection.

Music companies, book publishers, game companies, and film-makers are eager for us to check out their stuff, watch their films, play their games, or try their software. The more of their content we use, the more they get paid, pro rata. We still pay the same flat fee, unless we select some premium content—which we do all too often, we have to admit. It may cost only a dollar to "sit-in" on the latest recording sessions with your favorite artist, to order a copy of an issue of *Twilight Zone* that is not on the UMD Network, or to watch a special backstage Webcast of the Grammy awards. Our UMDs make media and entertainment content so irresistible that our cash just keeps flowing out on the network—a "dream come true" for any content provider that can get our attention.

The UMD service and its built-in tracking software allows the content providers and their agents to find out how their content is doing on the network—how many people have tried it, how many people have shared it, how many people have rated it, and who is talking about it. If we want to, we can share some, a little, or all of our data and other feedback with the UMD service, our friends, or the content providers themselves. We can also provide detailed feedback on their content and earn free UMD "points" that we can use to get free stuff. This way, some of our friends even make more money on the UMD network than they spend on getting the content! They review new bands, recommend new songs and movies to their peers, test new games, or become part of focus groups that evaluate new UMD services.

No longer are we tethered to our computer, the LAN connection, or the power plug. UMDs have become as commonplace as cell phones were a decade ago. Gone are the days of having to worry about where to get cool ring tones, how to turn the cell phone into a real gaming device, or where to watch our favorite soccer game.

The UMD comes fully licensed, and we can do whatever we want with it because most ways of using it are simply already included in the price of the device and related service fees. "Fair use" rules and, as customers, we really like the sense of empowerment. If we want access to special content, we simply use the various premium billing options that bill our UMD accounts, deduct directly from our electronic bank accounts, or use any of the cyber-cash services that we can subscribe to.

So what about the prices? It's 2015, and we're paying $59 a month to get all the basic content on the network for free, plus of course, thousands of minutes of free voice and videophone calls. Stream it, download it, listen to or view it on demand, transfer it, share it—whatever we want, anytime, anywhere. Peer-to-peer has taken on an entirely new meaning, and it smells like roses to the content providers and media companies.

Best of all, the sheer amount of content on the network is more than we could ever consume: more than five million music tracks from almost any record label, producer, or lately, directly from the artist. In addition, there are more than one million books; two hundred thousand movies, television shows, and video clips; twenty thousand games, and thousands of software packages. And we are talking about the good stuff here, not just back catalog and "archives."

These offerings are instantly available, instantly archived, book-markable, searchable with our content agents, and cross-referenced with our network buddies and friends.

The only thing we are really missing is the time to try it all!

Our Top-10 Truths
of the Music Business

Th<span></span>ese top-10 truths will guide the future of music, define the nature of the relationship between artist and fan, and likely prove to be of great significance to those in this business who wish to remain relevant. Our thinking is guided by our own experiences, and by hundreds of conversations we have had with all sorts of people working in the music business. Here, we examine the relationships and dynamics between the primary parties that make up the music industry: those who create the music, including artists, writers, and producers; those who market, deliver, and distribute it, such as the record companies and publishers; and the consumers and fans of music, who ultimately pay for it all.

1 **Music matters more than ever: the music market is alive and vibrant.**

By all accounts, more music has been consumed over the past five years than ever before. Again, music fans and "users" can thank the early digital music pioneers such as MP3.com and eMusic (www.emusic.com), as well as peer-to-peer ventures such as Napster, Kazaa, and Gnutella. They also owe a debt of gratitude to the hereto-unprotected CD format, which enables people to rip and burn CDs using personal computers. Billions of unprotected CDs have fueled the fire of digital song swapping.

Today, music fans are completely awash in music, and most are bombarded by music all day long. Anybody who wants to do so can stream, download, watch, edit, and cut and paste his own music, 24/7/365. File-sharing, transcoding (the art of turning an audio or video stream into a savable file), and online music have become the new "radio" for the digital generation. Music and the *music industry* are getting a lot of interest and attention, even though the *record industry* is on its way to the meat grinder. We are experiencing a phenomenal tidal wave of interest in music, and once that interest can be turned into better ways of discovering and enjoying music, the money will inevitably follow. Why mourn the *record* business when we will have much bigger fish to fry in the *music* business?

2 **The *record* business is not the same as the *music* business.**

This is a very important distinction to make. Many of us have been accustomed to thinking of the whole industry based on a simple formula: volume in CD sales = value of the industry. That is, fewer CD sales results in lower value. That is the myth, because, in fact, the record industry is a mere slice of the overall music industry pie—and many of the other slices are not even known to the average music fan. Music and event merchandising, concerts and touring, and live entertainment in general account for some $25 billion globally, while music publishing is a $12 billion business, approximately. Further, according to sources in *Pollstar*, *Billboard*, and *Music Week*, record companies make nearly $2 billion every year in "special products," such as give-away CD sets, corporate marketing items, and various business-to-business licensing activities.

What this means is that a musician does not have to be a recording artist or a performer to thrive in today's music industry. It means that you may be, at different times, a songwriter, lyricist, performer, band member, entertainer, promoter, entrepreneur, fashion designer, producer, teacher, or small business manager. Being a "creative" in the music business often means wearing several hats, doing several things at the same time, and picking up new skills on the fly. The sum of the income streams from these various activities make up the musician professional's compensation—and, of course, to be a successful musician, one must be an entrepreneur by nature, *and* operate as a business.

So, yes, the record business is suffering, but the music industry as a whole is alive and well.

3 The *artists* are the *brands,* and *entertainment* is the main attraction.

A record label is not usually a brand in its own right. The few exceptions—ECM Records, Def Jam, Motown, and perhaps Blue Note—prove the point. The artist and the record label are two entirely different things. It is the *artist's work* that everybody is interested in, while the label's identity, standing, and caché is a lesser concern for most fans—especially if the label is a large global corporation. Nobody buys a Britney Spears CD because BMG (formerly Zomba Records) puts it out, and few people cherish Columbia Records (Sony Music) because it's the home of Santana.

Prior to the 1920s, nearly every artist distributed their music "with their feet," determining who could listen to them by where they chose to perform. Artists, from medieval traveling minstrels to early Vaude-ville acts, knew their audiences personally, and interacted with them in many ways. They provided entertainment in the sitting rooms of manor houses, in churches, dances, plays, fairs, clubs, operas, street parties, birthdays, funerals, weddings, and other events. Music was not about packaging, distribution, or product sales. It was about live entertainment.

But despite the productization of music that the record industry created, most people still place the greatest value on their connection to an artist. We cherish particular artists because they are purveyors of feelings, special moments, experiences that we value. We create all manner of subliminal interactions with artists to whom we get attached. We track their whereabouts, we consider every work they put out, and we study the liner notes. We harbor deeply personal ties to them, often subconsciously, which is the prime reason for the strong economic pivot position of an artist. That puts the artist in a position of great power.

Today, the artist's contribution—talent, imagination, persona, and creative energy—is as important as ever. One could argue that digital technology has made it *easier* for artists to leverage their creativity, and if that is true, more music can be created in a shorter time, perhaps for a lower budget, with much less of the outside help that record labels traditionally provided. That makes the artist more powerful, and the average record label's offerings seem much less significant in compar-ison. Artists may no longer need the record labels' powerful checkbooks behind them. Music production facilities are increasingly affordable, small and mid-size marketing companies offer their services directly to artists, distribution options have grown by leaps and bounds, and managers and agents are taking more proactive roles.

Once the networked and technology-driven production and distribution channels are more readily available to the artist and their managers, the greatest strengths of the "old-style" record label (read: music company) will be in finance and in marketing—and even marketing can be effectively handled by small service organi-zations. One cannot, however, underestimate the importance of a strong business network, and record labels often have huge busi-ness networks, with a lot of mission-critical support just a phone call away. This networking power and high level of business connectivity will remain crucial—and will be one of the key assets of a successful musician business of the future.

New technology is encroaching on that turf, as well. Witness the blossoming of social/business networking tools, networked blogs, and "dating" applications such as Friendster, Ryze, and LinkedIn. Once these technologies become more widely used, one can expect that they will enable people to develop more extensive personal and business networks by "business dating and matching" online, as well as in follow-up, face-to-face events. Maybe then, the artist will no longer need to rely on their record label to gain access to a powerful business network. In fact, one can foresee a time not too far off when artists and their managers will fish in a huge pond of business connections that are nurtured in virtual and real-life conferences, tradeshows, and ultimately, marketplaces.

The remaining functions that a record label can fulfill clearly no longer warrant the steep financial, artistic, and personal premium that artists pay when they sign away their rights in a traditional recording contract. The old deal structures no longer make any sense for the artist—if indeed they ever did. A joint venture or co-op approach will be the way forward, and is already being explored by pioneering players in the record industry such as Sanctuary, EMI, and Artemis Records. As the business paradigms in general are morphing from "owning" to "sharing"—from product to service—so will the music industry be forced to go along. The artists who used to produce "work for hire" will now call on the former industry execs to be "hired to work." What a tremendous shift for all involved parties! Artists, if they want to, are shifting into a position of power in which they are working *with* the labels, not *for* the labels.

4 **Artists and their managers will shape the future.**
True to the public's perception, many musicians are fairly disorganized and habitually averse to strict order or tight organization. Being more on the creative side of things, artists are not always savvy or even interested in financial, marketing, or organizational matters. Frequently, this changes only after artists reach a certain standing that incentivizes them to take a good look at their financial situation. Mick Jagger, who for some time now has been keenly interested in the business affairs of the Rolling Stones empire, is a good example. A watertight

music business enterprise, the band has its own budgets, accountants, lawyers, bankers, and hardware and software to maintain its licensing, merchandising, touring, and investment enterprises.

Traditionally, managers and agents, as well as lawyers and accountants, have filled the administrative role, providing business services to musicians that could afford them. In the past ten years, managers have started to take on more and more duties, and this trend can only be expected to increase given the rapidly growing alienation between record companies and their artists. Certainly, the 2004 merger of the BMG and Sony Music will result in a good many executives being shown the door—but also, a lot of recording artists will be dropped, and this will fuel their managers' fires.

Associations such as the International Music Managers Foundation (IMMF) are poised to take the lead. Good managers will guide their artists through the myriad of choices they must make to remain in business and prosper. The artist/manager connection is very personal compared to a large record company's usual forty-three-acts-to-one-A&R-rep approach to artist management. Managers have an entirely different view on how they work with an artist and, by extension, how they get remunerated. Managers often get very low (if any) fixed income guarantees, at least initially, but in return may receive 15–25 percent of the artist's total revenues, which usually encompasses many of the available revenue streams.

Thus, managers have a more direct and immediate influence on all business decisions. Going forward, managers are likely to play a much bigger role as the central pivot point for business decisions, from publishing to marketing to touring and merchandising. Managers will lead the charge because their fame and fortune is directly linked to that of their artists. That can be a very favorable structure for the artist and leads to a much deeper level of cooperation than they would ever get from a traditional record label. Managers will select distribution channels, marketing agencies, public relations people, technology deals, and sponsorship packages. Smart managers will grow the new music economy by making their artists successful as independent musician businesses.

5 Publishing income is a crucial income stream.

Due to the complexity of a record deal and the usually lopsided terms contained therein, it is a known fact that publishing income tends to be a more valuable and reliable revenue stream than recording income—provided that the recording artist is also the songwriter. It just takes longer to build a good catalog of songs, and to get those songs into the right channels so that they are being used. Indeed, when the valuation was set for the recent acquisition of Warner Music Group, the publishing company was valued at $2 billion, compared with the $1.5 billion given for the recorded music operation.

In the U.S., a statutory mechanical royalty fee (currently ≅ 8.5 cents USD) is paid to the writers and their publishers, for every song on each CD that is sold, whether or not the writer is the performing/recording artist. In Europe, this fee is a fixed percentage of the published price-per-dealer (PPD), which usually amounts to a slightly higher amount. Public performance, synchronization (the use of a song in films, video, or advertising), and other song-related licensing incomes often provide substantial additional publishing revenue streams.

Keep in mind that the Internet and other digital networks are essentially giant publishing apparati—everything is about disseminating data (also known as "information" and "content"), getting heard or being viewed by people, and reaching out to others. Thus, publishers stand to profit greatly as technological advances enable the dissemination of data—if and when they learn to completely embrace it wholeheartedly and harness its power, rather than fight it, as many of their record company colleagues continue to do. Without a doubt, it benefits music publishers when their writers' works are disseminated as widely as possible, and digital networks can enable and monetize this like no other technology before. Once we can broaden our views on how the remuneration will be derived and start to embrace new models, the resulting revenues will be larger than ever before. One can see traces of this when looking at the flourishing ring-tone business, music for video games, and synchronization income that stems from digital media products.

Once copyright laws are amended to do what they were designed to do in the first place—protect authorship for a limited period of time so that an invention or work could be released to the public for the benefit of all—then the revenue floodgates will open, and publishers can truly harness the power of technology. Imagine the relief of reducing the importance of the good old mechanical reproduction license in favor of an "access license" that allows the public to freely use any song under a new blanket-license arrangement. The mechanical license was instituted along with the advent of the player piano as a statutory royalty on sales of piano rolls. Why would we want to hang on to a per-physical-copy payment paradigm in a digital world in which any given song can freely and without any real cost be reproduced? If the marginal costs of reproduction move towards zero, it is time to think of another way of measuring the "value" of a song—and there are many ways of doing that.

Once the mechanisms of performance royalty collection are adapted to address the new modes of song usage, music "renting," and distribution, performance royalty collection and publishing will take the lead as the primary source of compensation for musicians. Technologies such as the ones pioneered by Mediaguide, YesNetworks, and Yacast already allow us to monitor actual performance on broadcast networks with 99-percent accuracy, rather than relying on the sample-based accounting that has been commonplace until now. Under the existing structure, those who could afford it were able to individually audit performance logs, and because of the sampling-based system, they had a better chance of collecting royalties. The rich acts got richer while the smaller acts fell through the cracks. But now, we can pay each songwriter for the actual performance of their song on any monitored network. Ultimately, publishing will, by default, become inseparable from distribution. The tasks performed by what used to be "record labels" will be morphed into the publishing business—or perhaps we will see the birth of the next-generation music business.

6   Radio is no longer the primary way that people discover new music.

The days of mass-marketing records via playlist-homogenized broadcast radio stations are thankfully coming to a close. Talk radio began replacing music-centric radio some time ago. The playlists of the monolithic radio machines that do play music have, by and large, become a homogenous muck of sound-alikes, and the stations cater to advertisers more than they cater to listeners. In many ways, radio is simply a vehicle for advertising, much like network television. No single statement could be more telling than the one that appeared in

Fortune magazine, from former Clear Channel CEO Lowry Mays: "We're not in the business of providing well-researched music. We're simply in the business of selling our customers products."

Today, people are turning "off" to the radio as we know it, and "on" to the Internet, the cell phone, and to wireless and interactive technologies. Just as heavy 'Net users watch 38 percent less television, radio is losing out to digital media—or maybe it is morphing into it. Part of the reason for this is that music marketing and distribution are no longer intrinsically joined at the hip. Fans and consumers have far more convenient options for discovering new music than ever before, including the Internet, video games, television, and referrals from friends via e-mail, instant messaging, or social networks and user groups.

Digital music services such as iTunes, Musicmatch, Rhapsody, MSN, and Virgin Digital report that community features are major drivers of discovery for new music. Features such as swapping playlists with other people, or lists of the "top 10/20/100 most played songs," or "people who bought this also bought that" recommendations help fans discover new music online.

The big opportunity of the future is in finding a way to unobtrusively and effortlessly present new music. Radio as we know it will be replaced by digital music services that tie seamlessly into music distribution systems. Access and ownership will ultimately converge. If my digital "radio station" delivers my favorite playlists on demand—anytime and anywhere—the only reason I would accept another service would be that the service is more personal. It is likely that the very term "radio" will go the way of the word "record"—into the dustbin, or on to the digerati-wordsmiths to morph into the future.

Terrestrial radio in the U.S. is already threatened by consolidation, lack of diversity, and increasing censorship—just check out the declining stock prices for Clear Channel and Infinity for the last few years. As a means of introducing music to the masses, radio's effectiveness has been weakened as it has shifted to centralized playlists. Radio has also been under pressure from the FCC, with DJ Howard Stern being dropped from six markets by Clear Channel in response to heavy fines. We predict that consumers will not tolerate this kind of censorship in a world where any kind of programming is available on satellite radio or with a few taps of the computer keyboard.

Radio *as we know it* will become less relevant because people will have access to carefully programmed and custom-catalogued music anywhere, anytime. Digital music in its perfection is as good as the best radio ever was. Terrestrial radio will have to compete head to head with digital music services that deliver music via satellite or via wireless networks, just as television broadcasters compete against pay-per-view services and digital television providers.

What may keep radio attractive is the emotional connection forged through its people-factor, thus the appeal of talk radio. If radio wants to survive, it must retain the personal approach to presenting music and news, *but* must also embrace digital technologies, as the satellite radio networks Sirius and XM Radio are doing. And, it will have to adapt to being just one of the options available to people who are on the road.

7 Digital niche marketing outperforms mass marketing.

The idea that an artist has to sell more than five hundred thousand records to be successful is a bizarre myth propagated mostly by the music cartels that have to make up for the huge overhead they carry. *They* have to sell that many records to make money from any given artist, but *you,* as a musician business or small indie label, do not. If and when musicians can define their niche, truly differentiate themselves, and find efficient ways to reach out to people who are interested in their uniqueness, they can be successful on much smaller volumes reaching far fewer people. For each artist who has sold a million copies of a CD, there are hundreds that have done just fine by selling five thousand copies while keeping 80 percent of the income!

First of all, artists must embrace a more inclusive view of success—one in which great and long-lasting careers can be built on lower sales volumes of recorded music delivered directly, whether physically or digitally, from the artist to the fan. The artist can also recognize other ways of monetizing the artist/fan relationship. Without the record label as a go-between, artists can often maintain a greater degree of intimacy and involvement, and many stay in direct dialogue with their audiences.

The key to success in music niche marketing is to focus promotional dollars where they will bring the highest return—that is, maintain a low burn rate while getting the maximum results. To support this, technology can be developed to allow for the highest possible conversion rate from "interested user" to "buying customer." Matchmaking—having the right customer run across the "perfect" music at the right time—is where the art of marketing comes in. Finding the appropriate digital exposure channel, and determining when to start charging, and for what, will be the prime job for music marketeers of the future.

Once seeded and well-tended, niche markets can be extremely profitable, especially with intangible wares such as music. There is great opportunity in this sector, both for savvy new entrepreneurs, as well as for service and technology companies. In twelve to fifteen years, niche markets may bring in close to 40 percent of the global music revenues, and a new middle class of artists may finally thrive.

8 **Customers demand—and get—increasing convenience and value.**

For many years, people went to record stores to purchase songs heard on the radio; it was easy and convenient to purchase a record, tape, or CD at what appeared to be a reasonable price. Music still seemed like a good value. The cash flowed from the fans to the stores to the labels, and on to the artists, writers, and producers of the music. People liked the convenience of hearing new music on the radio—which, by the way, did feel like "free" to them—and in return being able to easily buy it at the record store. The CD was a music fan's favorite for the last twenty years because it is small, portable, easy to use, sounds great, is convenient to purchase, and, at the time, seemed to be worth the money.

Times have changed. Compared to the many burgeoning digital alternatives, the CD no longer seems like a "good value," and no longer looks as convenient. It simply does not have the same *relative value* in today's highly complex and competitive market . . . a market that offers alternative products such as DVDs, video games, cell phones, and digital cameras. And once the record industry shifts to copy-protected CDs that cannot be ripped to a computer's hard disk, you will see entire populations of music fans leave the CD behind, for good. Reading the myriad of press releases that deal with the efforts behind securing digital media sound carriers, one cannot help but wonder why anyone thinks that the average customer will have anything more than utter disgust for these kinds of newly restricted products. To get customers' attention, they'll have to put in some extra value in there, in return for the added security. After all, technology empowers users, and who could expect customers to step backwards and give up some of their rights?

Some consumers may well continue to purchase CDs or other fixed-media products for the foreseeable future—especially those who do not yet have suitable computers, PDAs, or powerful Internet connections, or those who prefer a high audio quality. But once it becomes exceedingly easy and cheap to acquire high-quality recordings in other zeros-and-ones ways, as it is via the 'Net, people will switch in droves. They will follow the path of convenience and value—a simple rule of business that has been proven time and time again. Water goes where it flows most easily.

Let's keep in mind that the Internet is only the first wave of development, only to be dwarfed by the explosion of wireless services. Broadband begets content begets broadband—once that snowball starts rolling, we will be utterly amazed at the velocity of content dissemination on digital networks. We may be able to plug a leak or two in the tightly guarded dams that hold back the rivers of content, but once the dam breaks, an unstoppable tidal wave will be unleashed. Rather than build more or better dams, let's build some fat channels for the easy flow of that content. Let's replace inefficient content-protection schemes with effective means of sharing-control and superdistribution!

On to the sacrifices . . . if observed objectively, the music industry has had the amazing luxury of earning billions of dollars every year, despite the fact the consumer has had to constantly sacrifice some essential needs and desires, simply to get any music at all.

Let us name a few of those quietly accepted and now deeply ingrained sacrifices: the impossibility of getting only a certain track by your favorite artist, without having to buy the entire album; the impossibility of getting any product from lesser-known artists if you do not live in the territory it is being distributed in; and the impossibility of getting an out-of-print recording. Until the 'Net came along, music consumers had seemingly resolved to sacrifice their real needs simply to get anything from the industry at all. A bird in the hand is worth two in the bush, right? But now, customers are empowered by digital networks, and are no longer content with making those sacrifices. They no longer shell out the cash without any further ado.

More often than not, the fast-moving entrepreneurs are the ones that can exploit this opportunity better than the incumbents. Much of this is already apparent today, but will indeed be the default mode tomorrow: any information about any artist and their work can be obtained, news spreads within minutes, downloads and streams are instantly available anywhere, anytime, and territorial restrictions become meaningless. To be sure, this is a boon for users and consumers—just like E-Trade, Amazon, Mapquest, Google, Yahoo, Expedia, and EasyJet. This trend is becoming so all-encompassing that, in the music business, we will see even more consumers simply refuse to accept those old limitations, and no longer be ready to sacrifice their rights to information on the altar of ancient industry rules and traditions. A huge change but also a huge opportunity— witness the tremendous success of companies like eBay, built entirely on customer empowerment, rather than sacrifice.

9 The current pricing model goes out the window.

Singles have never been even remotely profitable for the recording artist, and the new pay-per-track online models sported by iTunes, Rhapsody, BuyMusic, and others will ultimately fare no better. Apple reports that some of iTunes downloads are for complete album packages, at album prices, but it will be very difficult to keep digital album prices up at $10-12 when the novelty wears off. The bottom line is that selling the content is very unlikely to be the main method of bringing revenue to the coffers of digital music services. Our hunch is that as much as 50 or 60 percent of the future revenues will come in from selling other products and services, and from advertising, sponsorship, and marketing tie-ins. The music itself may often only be the default ingredient in the mix, rather than the sole purpose of the transaction. The days of making lots of money from selling 100 percent "content" are over for music.

As a consequence, the traditional thinking behind recording contracts no longer applies and needs to be completely overhauled; the 1950s model is obscenely outdated in today's environment. If you consider the very nature of a digital, intangible, and limitlessly-repeatable transaction, the artist deserves a great deal more of

the revenue than the 8 to 15 or even 20 percent that they theoretically would get *if* the record company accounting was fair, *if* sales
were accurately reported, and *if* there were not all of these deduc-
tions and recoupable costs in their contracts. This plantation-style
proposition ("You work—I own") is an insult to today's artist, and it
is being rapidly abandoned in favor of a more balanced approach
that marries the convenience and value of digital music with the
consumers' hunger for music, in a way that actually makes sense for
tomorrow's artists and fans.

Today, in larger and larger numbers, music fans are expressing
their disdain for the way that music is priced and the endless mara-
thon of obstacles that they encounter when looking to buy music.
They are becoming aware that the record companies want them to
pay somewhere between six to fifteen times what the artist makes
from the sale of the CD. It is becoming clear that this is a very inefficient way of distributing music when one considers how much is paid
and to whom, in order to get the true value of the transaction, namely
the music. Customers fire up their Internet connections, and live out
that deep lust for the sharing of music. Their message is: "You're not
giving me what I want at a reasonable price, so I am going elsewhere."

We need to exploit the current ways that people learn about,
select, legitimately acquire, and listen to music. We need to reflect the
reality of the digital marketplace, not the reality of the '60s and '70s.
The game has changed. In order to have a business that can thrive
and blossom, we must consider the interests of the fans and artists
first, and the existing incumbents' business interests second.

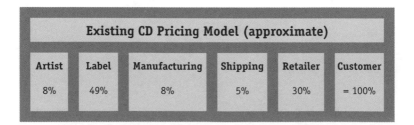

Existing CD Pricing Model (approximate)					
Artist	Label	Manufacturing	Shipping	Retailer	Customer
8%	49%	8%	5%	30%	= 100%

Today's pricing scheme will be ripped to pieces by the deep habit
changes within the music-fans' cultures, and by ever-increasing
competition from other entertainment products. Consumers that

have figured out how to get music free, like water, from the seemingly bottomless digital wells—legal or not—will not be persuaded to continue paying for the "Evian" that is today's CD. The current pricing will be replaced by a very potent liquid pricing system that incorporates subscriptions, bundles of various media types, multi-access deals, and added-value services. And, it will uphold the fair-use provisions that the customer is used to, such as the right to share and the right to resell. After all, it has proven to be impossible to make significant technological leaps, and yet take backward steps as far as user rights are concerned.

We will likely see additional relatively small "fees" that all consumers must make in order to get some basic service. Similar levies, taxes, or bundled-in fees are likely to be established for basic content services that will be available on digital networks, such as for wireless carriers, WiFi providers, and ISPs, with the caveat that they are likely to be very incremental and thus not an obvious burden to the individual user. Imagine if all of the 1.4 billion cell phone users around the world paid only one dollar each, per month, to get access to a basic music service. This would already amount to half the value of worldwide CD sales, per year. Not very realistic with today's music moguls, but very likely tomorrow, indeed.

Beyond this the consumer can choose from a variety of good-value "package deals" and "choice payments" such as premium subscriptions, memberships, donations, and pay-per-view offerings. All in all, once the pricing models have changed and music can flow freely, we may see up to 80 percent of the population in the leading markets become active music consumers. Compare this with the today's average 10–15 percent that actually buys any music, on physical media, and you can sense the profit potential of this fundamental shift.

10 **Music is mobile, and new models will embrace a more liquid view of music.**

Music wants to be mobile and moveable; this has been a sticking point with music fans all along. The gramophone was not very conducive to mobility, the Walkman was a huge success because it was mobility objectified, the CD's success was also about mobility, and digital music represents the very pinnacle of the mobility paradigm. If we define mobility as the ability to access music from anywhere anytime, as the ability to take it with you without undue burden, and as the ability to exchange music with others, we have the very definition of digital music. The only way this can move is up!

The music industry may need to look at some of the tactics employed by video game developers and software manufacturers: create products that are "try first, then buy," as well as upgradeable, and develop an ever-expanding array of services and products or formats in which to sell their product: bundling, repackaging, and co-marketing. Recorded music has too long been viewed as a "static" product rather than a more fluid or participatory entertainment experience—but the latter is where its real value lies. One can already get a glimpse of that theory at work when looking at the various digital music ventures that deliver recorded concerts immediately after the show, such as Instant Live, Disc Live, eMusic Live (formerly DCN), Livephish.com, and LiveMetallica.com.

The process and pace of new releases needs to be synchronized with new means of product development and new niche-marketing activities. Fortunes will be made by those who know "the secret ingredients," who truly understand what all involved market participants want, and who can envision the appropriate technological tools to deliver the services to them.

Multi-access to music will rapidly become the default setting in the future, allowing consumers to "fill up" their music devices using wireless as well as fixed-media or on-demand manufacturing services at gas stations, train stations, shopping malls, juke boxes, and coffee shops. Mobile phones as we know them today will be replaced by infinitely more powerful mobile communication and entertainment solutions that can network seamlessly and effortlessly. Mobile music players will connect to digital music services using GPRS, UMTS, Bluetooth, and WiFi-type connections, and will be able to stream or download music content, in addition to serving as mobile phones, PDAs, mobile gaming stations, and social software platforms. Mobile music systems will support interactivity between users, enabling playlist sharing and other community features.

Storage power will be virtually unlimited, with devices supplying up to 1 terabyte of storage within the next two to three years. Flat-fee access deals, cheap international roaming, and "content and connectivity" bundles will make mobile music offers virtually irresistible.

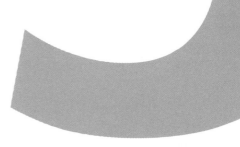

Futurizing Some Popular Music Industry Myths

In this chapter, we will expose five of the most common myths about the music business. These widely held mind-twists are the reason that, a whopping fifty years after Elvis, not a whole lot has changed—that is, until just a few years ago, with the advent of the Internet, MP3, Napster, and file-sharing. Back in the '50s and '60s, the music business was a relatively simple business to run, and very, very few people knew what really went on behind the scenes. Now, getting access to detailed information is a mouse-click or an instant message away, and the distorted business practices of the music business have been laid bare.

The Internet, and digital technologies in general, make it much harder to conceal the facts: now, more of the truth has come to the surface, artists speak out publicly, everyone can read about it, and big changes are already resulting from that. This kind of informational transparency in a business context creates clarity, and it also creates a certain amount of pressure, both of which usually translate into advantages for the consumer. As author William Gibson writes, now, "In the age of the leak and the blog, of evidence extraction and link discovery, truths will either out or be outed, later if not sooner. This is something I would bring to the attention of every diplomat, politician, and corporate leader: the future, eventually, will find you out." And this reality becomes more relevant with every day that we progress into a digitally networked society.

Just like the times following the invention of the printing press, the automobile, and the television, the technological advancement of the Internet has initially turned things upside down. We will go through this period of considerable creative chaos until the new technology becomes *truly* useful for the average person. The good news is that we are getting there; the bad news is that the transition is going to be painful for a lot of people.

1 Myth 1. Music is a product.

Part of the reason that the music industry is in such sorry shape these days is that the people who control the "old" industry have convinced themselves that they *are* the music business, and that success in music means distributing products that they must control—that only *they* can deliver, properly market, and turn a profit on. They not only believe their own public relations; they have become it!

Have you ever wondered why we have rivers of undistinguish-able, shrink-wrapped music oozing at us from radio and television? It is because record companies think they sell products, MTV shows products, retailers display products, and we consumers have been willingly buying these products. Nice and simple—easy to control, and easy to manipulate. Sell singles, sell albums, sell CDs, sell downloads.

Let's define a product as something that is made or created by a person or machine, especially something that is offered for sale. Is that what music is all about? Is music a product? Is it only something that you can "make a substantial profit on?" We think not. Music is a combination of entertainment, communication, and passion, an ephemeral occurrence, something intangible, and something that is experienced in everyday life. Music today is proliferating and expanding at an unprecedented rate. Music-making is a global phenomenon, and there is more of it being made than ever before. There are more bands, more writers, more songs, more CDs, more shows, and more awareness of all of it.

That is what is making it so hard today to duplicate the success of mega-artists like Madonna, Michael Jackson, and the Who: there are too many choices, too many different ways to get music, and of course, too many other interesting ways to spend money. In other words, consumers are starting to leave the narrow confines of the turf that the purveyors of media wanted them to stay in, and *diversity* is ruining the plan that worked so well for so many years.

When the first vinyl records hit the market in 1915, the music business as we think of it today barely existed. Music was dancing, cabaret, sing-alongs, band concerts, eventually radio, and instru-mental performance. People didn't "own" music; they listened to it, experienced it, and enjoyed it.

During the past hundred years or so, we turned musicians, performers, and even ideas into "products," and from that, have narrowed everything down to a simple formula: you write a song that sounds unique to you (note that uniqueness gets harder and harder to achieve, given the millions of already existing songs), you register it as yours, you exploit it exclusively, and make a ton of money. Of course, this goes nicely along with the idea that the prime method of exploitation is the sale or use of physical copy or product.

But wait a minute. Isn't this supposed to be the "entertainment" business? Isn't music a form of entertainment, meant for enjoyment and pleasure by all? We define entertainment as "something that amuses, pleases, or diverts, especially a performance or show." Most artists love to hear, play, and participate in music. They play music because, along with loving it themselves, they love to make an impact on the audience. They love expressing themselves and making people *feel* things. Isn't that what music is all about?

The distorted view of music as a product is a manifestation of the late Industrial Age, when companies were able to fix music in time on sound carriers, then control and exploit it to their benefit. We consumers were brainwashed into believing that we have to "own" the music in order to enjoy it. Purchasing records or CDs is a way of "tagging" the music that we like in order to be able to listen to it later. But the digital networks are beginning to change this equation. Access to music will replace ownership of it. We have passed through the Industrial Age to the Information Age, and music will never be the same again.

Take, for example, the exploitation of images as products. Prior to approximately 1900, images were created by hand or reproduced via various means of printing, and their distribution was secure and controlled. About the same time that music became a "product," still-picture cameras, such as the 35mm, became popular. Photography developed into a popular hobby and grew exponentially as a profession, both at the same time. Around 1945, the Polaroid camera was introduced. Ever since, photographic acquisition, development, and processing have become increasingly sophisticated, culminating in today's digital photography boom. If the entities that controlled the distribution of images in the late 1890s had acted like today's record companies, and tried to prevent the exploitation of their images via photographic and digital means, we would not have the rich web of commercial activities that we have today in the areas of photography, image processing, filmmaking, videography, and computer graphics.

This is where the idea of "music as a service" can come in. Economically speaking, music will be bigger than ever before, once we free music from the shackles of having to be a product. In other words, free music from having to contain at least twelve tracks of a certain length in a certain style throughout all tracks, and out in the stores in a particular country by a certain date—and the true potential of music will explode, digitally *and* physically, in atoms, bytes, and dollars.

As we have witnessed in photography and the video/film businesses, new technologies make the industry "pie" larger, not smaller. A music industry that fashions itself as a service industry is likely to be many times larger than the product-based system that we have today. We will still have some physical products (likely in new formats), but we will have a vast number of additional digital music products and services available to us. However, the rules of the game will change, and the current companies that are still in control of the ship will need to let go in order for everyone to prosper.

Of course, this is where it gets ugly. The end of "music as a product" may mean the end of the record label as we know it. This is what today's struggle is all about. Record labels, as we know them, can only survive without drastic changes if music *remains* a product, and they are fighting tooth and nail for survival. They want to keep it as it was, in a scenario of self-annihilation before surrender. They are fighting not just for economic reasons but also for a way of life. Going even further, in a 2004 statement, Jack Valenti, the former Motion Picture Association of America (MPAA) president and old compatriot of the folks over at the Recording Industry Association of America (RIAA), says, "Companies have a responsibility to develop products that operate within the letter of the law and do not expose their customers to illegal activities." So now, ISPs, telecommunication companies, and software companies are responsible for the use of their products? And, to bring this to its logical extreme, gun makers should be held responsible for the deaths of thousands of people?

Valenti went much further when talking about the fair-use rights of the consumer. He told the Associated Press in November 2003, "If you buy a DVD, you have a copy. If you want a backup copy, you buy another one." By extension, then, if you lose your iPod with that $4,000-worth of iTunes songs on it, you'll just have to buy them again? Long live customer empowerment!

Products are nice and clean, and thus the labels can merrily segment, productize, synergize, and market the "stuff" until the cows come home. This unabashed product-centric philosophy has led us down a path on which musicians and writers are being meat-packaged into a fixed medium, with 90 percent of their true power and meaning stripped away, and the remaining 10 percent sold as "the real thing" to line the pockets of people who have positioned themselves at the gates.

Before musicians were placed in front of enormous gramophone-recording funnels and asked to cut down their performance to an acceptable and packageable length, music was essentially an ephemeral art; you had to be there to hear it. These very same musicians were performing in hotels, bars, concert halls, churches, private homes, and on the street. Some were held in very high esteem, and a rare few were wealthy—if they were really good and if their message came across. The economics for musicians were not all that different than they are today.

One has to look no further than some so-called "developing" countries such as India to see how this is still working today. In India, there is a huge amount of illegal CD manufacturing, and very few "paid" music products are being sold—yet India has one of the most vibrant music scenes you could imagine. It just doesn't have a very wealthy legitimate record *industry*. The same goes for Jamaica, Cuba, and Nigeria.

Will people stop making music because it can no longer be sold mainly as a product? No way. The labels and publishers want us to believe so, but the truth is far from it. In the July 7, 2003 edition of *The New Yorker* magazine, Chris Blackwell, founder of Island Records, is quoted as saying, ". . . the people you are trying to reach, by and large, don't view music a commodity but as a relationship with a band." Right on, Chris—and that is what it is all about, and what technology can give (back) to us: meaningful, direct relationships with artists and bands, as a service.

The product-mantra is also at work when the music industry sues their customers for not playing by the rules, as is happening at the time of this writing, and is very likely to continue to happen for quite some time. From college students to grandmothers, children, and Navy shipmen, watch out everyone, because the music and recording industry is coming after you if you dare to question the almighty product mantra! We will sue you into submission. Either buy the product at the prices we dictate, or go to jail.

We think this is all wrong. We are going to suggest new ways of working. Let's borrow Brian Eno's simple mantra, outlined in *Wired* in 1995—"It's the process, not the product"—and watch it finally come to fruition.

2 **Myth 2. File-sharing is killing the music industry.**
There is no direct proof that file-sharing itself is hurting the overall music industry. The record companies are touting this single-bullet theory to explain away all the ingrained problems of an antiquated business reaching the end of its life cycle. Indeed, one can argue that file-sharing, an extraordinarily popular activity, is the cheapest form of music marketing there ever was.

According to Danny Goldberg, Chairman and CEO of Artemis Records, on *Frontline* (2004):

> You know, I don't think there was any more downloaded song than 50 Cent's last year (2003), and yet it sold nine million albums. So there were nine million households that felt, despite the fact that they had seen the video, despite the fact that they could get it online, that they wanted to hear the full statement that 50 Cent was making.

On a global scale, traditional piracy is certainly impacting the music industry. First, however, let's define the meaning of the word "piracy," because the confusion starts there. Traditionally, in the music business, piracy refers to the activities of organized criminals who manufacture illegal copies of CDs, DVDs, tapes, and records, then photocopy the covers and sell the illicit product on the street for a steep profit. Pirates in many countries run pressing plants that churn out CDs by the millions without paying the rights holders, i.e., without paying the mechanical reproduction licenses and mechanical license fees to the owner of the master recordings. (In most countries, these licenses are administered by the Mechanical Rights Organizations (MROs) such as GEMA in Germany, or JASRAC in Japan.)

The International Federation of the Phonographic Industry estimates that the number of illegally copied and/or manufactured CDs climbed 14 percent in 2002 and an additional 4.3 percent in 2003, to 1.1 billion units—and 35 percent of all CDs sold, globally, are illegal copies. It is estimated that the value of the pirated music sold amounts to $4.6 billion, and these figures do not even include online file-sharing or "transcoding" (recording) of audio streams. In 2002, the global recorded music market dropped 7 percent to $32 billion, and another 7.6 percent in 2003. CD piracy, as defined above, could account for the majority of the drop in CD sales all by itself.

Now, do people who trade MP3 files via the fifty-plus existing file-sharing networks fit in the very same definition of piracy? We contend that there is a vast difference here. Yes, it is (currently) illegal to trade files, but where is the profit motive that underlies piracy? Maybe these file-traders simply are serious music enthusiasts who lack any compelling commercial alternative to getting their need for music fulfilled. Let's face it: CDs are just too expensive these days. They are nearly the same price as DVDs, which are a richer, more costly, and technically sophisticated forms of media. And these file traders must be quite serious about their mission, indeed, to put up with the countless problems that they encounter when downloading music from the peer-to-peer file-sharing networks.

What's more, is this done with evil intent? Are they looking to inflict pain on the artist or the record company, or do they want to ruin the industry? Certainly not. The fifty million or more people who share music over the Internet want to acquire music cheaply, get connected to other people, share with them, learn about new music, and have instant access to what they want and where they want it. The radio no longer delivers enough new music to satisfy. Technology has given them a turbo-charged version of tape-swapping, an activity that has been extremely popular in the past and has fueled the advance and promotion of many successful bands, including the Grateful Dead, Metallica, Phish, and countless others.

Is file-sharing on P2P networks really free? People pay a lot of money for computers, modems, DSL lines, and monthly ISP charges to access this "free" music, along with the myriad of other online content and services.

Consider, for a moment, what do these "willful infringers" actually get when they trade files on the P2P networks, today? We are talking about files that, for the most part, sound a lot worse than a track off a CD, may be encoded incorrectly or cut off early, via downloads that are canceled in mid-transmission, that lack any or all correct meta-data, and on and on. Are the people who do this (i.e., almost everyone we seem to know) pirates, just like those organized counterfeit CD factories run by Russian CD mafias and neighborhood gangs in big cities across the U.S. and around the world? Criminals? Destined for jail? We hardly think so.

In the music industry, we have been subjected to a constant barrage of assertions that the free, uncontrolled downloading of music is the main cause of the industry's troubles. This is preposterous. Today, in full consideration of the current "jail the file sharers" campaigns that the RIAA et al are promoting, we have nothing but another round of oligopoly-led McCarthyism—perhaps some of the last, absurd twitching of Big Music, AKA the major record labels. Did you download a track without regard to our restrictions? Did you "dare to share?" Did you dare to be curious about new music? Did you want to save another artist from obscurity? Did you stop needing us for your music? Bad boys and girls!

Whether the rampant downloading of music hurts the music industry or whether it could indeed help it to grow is ultimately an irrelevant question. You might as well ask if cell phones hurt the landline phone companies, if Xerox machines hurt book sales, if the fax machine hurts the postal service, if WiFi hurts Internet service providers, or if no-flat car tires hurt AAA's towing services. The answer doesn't matter; the point is that technology moves forward anyway, if and when it is meaningful to people, easy to use, respectful of human nature, readily available, and easily and widely affordable.

Tens of millions of people are trading music online—sixty million in the U.S., alone, at the time of this writing. More than five hundred million users have downloaded the various software programs that enable file-sharing, and many more join the party every minute. The adoption of P2P software has been faster than any other technology adoption before, faster than the telephone, the PC, and the Internet itself. And the record industry wants to stop this by suing its own customers?

Finally, let's remember that cable television started as piracy. That's right: 85 percent of all Americans today pay for something that used to be pirated. When cable initially became available, the first programs were simply captured terrestrial broadcasts that were rebroadcast at different times. Talk about lawsuits! Finally, the Supreme Court decided that it was not illegal or a violation of copyright to capture and rebroadcast terrestrial television, but that a compulsory license fee had to be paid. And what do we have today? Cable television is a booming business, everybody has more choices, and most everybody pays a fee.

So why are we still wondering if file-trading can hurt or help the music industry? What are the powers-that-be looking to do? Turn off the Internet, blow it up, penalize the use of it, booby-trap it, and litigate people out of existence? This strikes us as utterly Orwellian, ridiculous, and shortsighted. The music business is long overdue for restructuring, to be kicked in the rear, to go fish for some true innovations, and to reinvent itself. This restructuring has begun. The party is over. Rather than point fingers and litigate to preserve something that time has passed, try this: innovate, adapt, or die. This has long been the rule in many other industries, so maybe it's about time that the music industry's grace period expires?

3. Myth 3. Copyright is linear, and ideas can be owned.

So many questions pop up on our radar, when looking at copyright issues. Isn't a certain amount of creative chaos and freedom required to create new things? Shouldn't creators have license to be inspired and, to a certain degree, borrow freely? Who owns the English language, and could they charge us license fees? Who owns the idea of how to make a wheel? Isn't every creator standing on the shoulders of giants, somehow? Hasn't Walt Disney himself taken quite liberally from the brothers Grimm to create his icons of modern cartoonism, and did he not get inspiration for the Mickey Mouse cartoon *Steamboat Willy* from Buster Keaton's rendition of *Steamboat Bill, Jr.*?

After all, neither culture nor art are made in a vacuum. Rather, they are always a blend of many influences, some of which are utterly new, some very ancient. Should we not be able to take the pieces we need, give credit where it's due, and move on to creating something new? Where will a system lead that restricts a pyramid of innovation, inch by inch, year after year?

As technology moves forward at a breathtaking pace, Metcalf's "law of the exponentiality of networks" and Moore's "law of the pace of innovation" are feeding off of each other. Metcalf says that the power of a network is exponential to its number of users—witness the first Napster, or Hotmail, or Skype—while Moore says that the power of processing approximately doubles every eighteen months.

As evidence of this, people are getting used to digital technology and to freely and effortlessly trading music, films, art, texts, and other documents. And because music is digital, it can be easily produced, copied, and transferred, and it can be easily adapted, modified, and transformed. Any given piece of digital music can quickly be borrowed, mutated, sampled, morphed, and adapted into a new piece, and this practice tests the assumptions that underpin copyright law and the nature of ownership.

Consider a world where copyright holders had complete and perpetual control of their works. The following article from the parody Web site, The Onion (www.theonion.com), illustrates this nicely:

> Lawyers for Dr. Henry Heimlich, inventor of the Heimlich maneuver, warned Monday that the doctor will sue anyone who performs his patented procedure without paying royalties. "The Heimlich maneuver is a registered trademark of my client," attorney Steve Greene said. "We are prepared to protect Mr. Heimlich's proprietary rights, even if it means filing a legal injunction against any non-royalty-paying choking victims."

In such a world, claims of intellectual property would be unthinkable, since nearly every action and thought would infringe upon somebody else's claims of ownership, and one would therefore be perpetually guilty of property violations.

Consider the life of copyright: given the increasingly explosive pace of life and the imminent arrival of content superdistribution, one would expect that the term of copyright—that is, how long a copyright stays in effect—would be continuously reduced, but the opposite has happened. The term of copyright has been extended not less than twelve times in the past forty years, and now stands at "life of creator plus seventy-five years." This is brought to you mostly courtesy of Big Mouse (AKA Disney), and self-proclaimed copyright crusaders such as the late Sonny Bono.

However, the U.S. copyright rules impact countless other "unique" copyrighted works. Since a digital copy of a media object is exactly like the original, but does not in any way deplete it or remove it from further use, one can hardly compare this to the world of physical goods, where the use or possession of a product actually removes the possibility of someone else owning the very same product. In the digital content realm, ultimately, how can we make a scarce resource of something that in reality is infinite?

For example, what is happening to our right to be inspired? How can I be inspired by somebody else's work, and build something new "on top of it," when I cannot even refer to, quote, or use a tiny sample of it? How can I take in all this content that floats around me, that surrounds me everywhere, and then not avail myself of any of it, in any way, until seventy-five years after the death of the author? Even the tiniest sample of someone else's work could get me in deep trouble.

The people who profit most from the repeated extension of the term of copyright are the de facto copyright owners—the media companies and publishers, the commercial owners or quasi-owners of the rights—and not necessarily the actual creators of the works. The U.S. Constitution says that Congress can grant copyrights to "authors," but these rights seem to have been licensed, morphed, and extended to create a virtual monopoly on creativity, with only a handful of some very large companies owning huge chunks of the cultural and artistic output of the past fifty years, and doing everything they can to milk more immediate profits out of it.

Stanford University Professor Lawrence Lessig, one of the most brilliant minds in this turf, has written extensively about the dangers of letting copyright law run unchecked into the future. Lessig's Creative Commons (www.creativecommons.org) has developed a variety of licenses that provide a greater degree of freedom in the use of a work, as in "some rights reserved." Lessig cautions us to examine the motives of the RIAA and the content industry's war on piracy, and argues against the larger movement on the part of the media industry to "remake the Internet, before it remakes them."

Some 2004 U.S. legislation proposals, heavily sponsored and lobbied for by the film, music, and entertainment industries, threaten to limit the rights of individuals to acquire and trade content online. One bill, the Pirate Act, introduced by U.S. Senators Patrick Leahy and Orin Hatch, provides the U.S. Justice Department with both federal and civil penalties to bring against people found using peer-to-peer technology to download music. Both Leahy and Hatch have received hundreds of thousands of dollars in campaign contributions from the entertainment industries. Another proposal, called the Inducing Infringement of Copyrights Act, from U.S. Senators Hatch, Bill Frist, Tom Daschle, and Barbara Boxer, would allow entertainment companies to target any company that "intentionally induces" people to violate copyrights. The lawmakers claim that this proposal would let them go after the peer-to-peer software manufactures, but a broader interpretation of it could apply to MP3 players like the iPod, personal computers, CD burners, and CDR discs. Both of these bills pit the content owners against the technology providers to the overall detriment of the consumer, and both threaten our rights as individuals.

"It's unfortunate that the entertainment industry devotes so much energy supporting punitive efforts at the federal and state level, instead of putting energy into licensing their content for P2P distribution so those same people could be turned into customers," says Philip Corwin, attorney for Sharman Networks (Kazaa) in a *Wired* news article. "The Pirate Act effectively gives government the authority to use taxpayer dollars to bring civil actions against file sharers on behalf of copyright holders."

All involved parties need to carefully consider any new legislation regarding copyright, not just the corporate attorneys from entertainment companies like Universal and Disney, or even the Beatles. The fundamental problem is that on the Internet, every use essentially creates a copy, and content becomes amorphous and thus ubiquitous. As Lessig argues, because every act of consumption on the Internet creates a copy, various laws suddenly regulate each of these acts. This is totally unlike the acts I can undertake under the concept of fair use with physical property such as books and CDs, which one can freely lend, copy, and resell, at least to a very large degree. This dilemma creates the need for less restrictive legal environments, as far as digital music is concerned.

Since the original drafting of the U.S. Constitution, extensive redrafting of copyright laws by armies of corporate lawyers has greatly inhibited artistic innovation by preventing new artists from making easy use of past innovations, and first and foremost from being directly inspired by the masters of the past. Having too many limitations on public domains is not beneficial for anyone on the creative side. It only favors the media giants that benefit from the immediate extension of their copyrights.

Indeed, the original concept of copyright was developed to allow the author of a work a chance to exploit their work for a very limited period of time (five to eight years), and not forever. The grandfathers of copyright did not provide any protection for derivative works; this idea came into play much later. Taken to its logical extreme, the current definition of copyright implies that all rock songwriters should pay licenses to somebody for hijacking the blues and building upon it. Likewise, all of today's popular grunge bands could end up owing royalties to Nirvana, Soundgarden, and Pearl Jam for their part in initiating a new genre, right?

In our view, today's copyright law does not differentiate sufficiently between distributing a literal copy of someone else's work, and building on the work of others to create a new work based in part on what had come before. Surely this does little to stimulate creativity, when the only works that can be legitimately copyrighted cannot be based in any way on any previously copyrighted work without permission. The natural process of creation just does not work this way—just ask Bob Dylan or the Beatles.

This is not to say that there should be less compensation to the authors whose works are borrowed from, or at the very least some attribution as to the source. A challenge for the future is to find ways to better measure and report the commercial uses of a given work, now that all this technology is available. Today, commercial uses of a work are monitored via permissions from the authors, but tomorrow's system could be based on a more fluid flow of knowledge and ideas, and the sharing across some form of alternate, contributory compensation system.

A growing number of projects are already stretching the boundaries of copyright and pushing the limits of "creative ingenuity." Artist Jay-Z recently launched a high-profile experiment when he released the a cappella vocal raps from his *Black Album,* and challenged producers and remix artists to remake the entire album. Before long, there were dozens of remixes available on the 'Net, including the now infamous *Grey Album,* a sonic remix of Jay-Z and the Beatles' *White Album.* EMI, who distributes the Beatles' sound recordings, sent DJ Danger Mouse, the remixer, a cease-and-desist letter about the time that more than one million copies of the *Grey Album* had been downloaded. The *Grey Album* may indeed be the most popular album ever to be delivered exclusively online to date, without the benefit of major label distribution or any marketing budget whatsoever. You can make your own remix at the Jay-Z Construction Set Web site (www.jayzconstructionset.com).

The Beatles and their affiliated companies have been some of the most litigious musicians ever. They have even sued each other and fought over rights in countless lawsuits brought against unauthorized users of their works. They have steadfastly refused to license their music for most soundtracks and compilations, and they vigorously defend their rights when samples are used. They have even sued Apple Computer, Inc. multiple times over the use of the Apple name, apparently for getting into the music business and inventing iTunes and the iPod. Yet, the Beatles borrowed heavily, and rather obviously, in some cases, from rock-and-roll pioneers such as Buddy Holly. One can recount numerous interviews in which they readily admitted to their influences. So just where do you draw the line? Are the Beatles just plain lucky that Muddy Waters, the Everly Brothers, and Chuck Berry didn't have armies of attorneys at their disposal at the time?

Good artists borrow, great artists steal.

—Generally attributed to Pablo Picasso

Another problem with the linear concept of copyright, and the idea of *owning* a given copyright exclusively and pretty much forever, is that it's based on the idea that any given work is forever a finished product. This is an extremely Western viewpoint, of course, and we feel that this definition of a "work" is much too narrow. At best, one could argue that a piece of music is finished for now or for a while, and that during this time, it deserves a chance to be attributed to the creator, to allow him or her to tap into the flow of monies that may come from it.

Copyright was originally conceived to protect the writers and publishers of books and prevent flagrant plagiarism—but can the very same concept of copyright really be applied to an art that's more fluid, such as music? Is a piece of music ever really finished, or "frozen," as long as it is being continually performed? As we can see with many folk songs, music has a tendency to continually morph and change with each musician that performs it over time. If it's not a fixed, static product, it then becomes nearly impossible to define, never mind to own and control. In a sense, when it's not ownable, it is really no one's perpetual property—or perhaps it is everyone's property.

The best thing we, as creators, could hope for, then, would be to have a reasonable period of time during which all derivative versions would need to pay their respect to our "original," an original that is likely to have been inspired by other people's originals, of course. During this reasonable period of time, we would get to benefit directly from that protection. In our view, this window would need to be adjusted to reflect the speed of society in general, of course, since a faster-moving world is likely to make faster use of entertainment content.

In many other cultures, music is often considered a perpetual work in progress, and therefore never really owned by any one partic- ular person. In those cultures, exclusive, personal ownership gives way to a sense of communal ownership—and in this kind of society, a musician's income is derived not from the sale of a product, but from the musician's position in the chain of performers/creators and, of course, from his position in society in general. The creator benefits not from his exclusive claim of ownership, but from his personal contribution to the communal experience of the music.

In the traditional societies of Ghana, for example, many songs are based on local "libraries" of rhythmic and melodic patterns, most of which are taught to every single member of the community, and some of which end up in almost all songs. Who's to say, then, who the original inventor of that phrase was? Was it one person, a particular chieftain, a group, a tribe? Of course, that question is rarely asked in a society in which music is not a product, i.e., a property that can be owned. Instead, a particular rhythm may be considered collectively owned, or a common inheritance—but then again, few people in that community are trying to make money from selling music products.

"So what?" you may argue. Who cares about these traditional communal societies and their understanding of intellectual property? There is no substantial music business in those communities anyway! Well, you may be surprised to hear that the very same ownership issue arises in a lot of Americana music, including bluegrass, old- time fiddle music, and in American jazz. Who really "invented" the I VI II V chord progression that is at the heart of hundreds of popular folk and pop songs? Who wrote the old spirituals that Bill Monroe sings? Where did Robert Johnson get his songs from—the public domain, other musicians, or the devil himself—as the tale goes? And how much of popular music is based on the works of the past? How's this for a future scenario: With technology turning the entire world into everyone's coffeehouse, we can disseminate and exchange ideas very quickly, the "morphing" process is instantaneous, and we can stand on each other's shoulders much more easily. Given the sheer velocity and viral character of that process, and the potentially huge number of participants, it will prove impossible to claim a long-term ownership of and lock on creative ideas, be they music, art, business, technology, or otherwise. We will likely need to get used to the fact that copyright is *becoming* nonlinear, that the pace of exploitable ideas has vastly accelerated, and that most content, media, and art is never finished because the *process* itself is also part of the "art." If this sounds a lot like Marshall McLuhan's famous philosophy, "the medium is the message," . . . well, it is!

We will have to accept that the current copyright regime—and it is most certainly a regime—is not a default requirement for creators who want to make a living of their art. We must recognize that other models exist that do not abridge fair-use principles and can still turn over some very real money. (We will explore these in upcoming chapters.) In the future, creators can and will monetize their creative output much more quickly and effectively than they do today, without the use and the legal underpinnings of vastly outmoded canons of copyright law. And, they won't have to encounter the legions of lawyers that seek to enforce it. Then, think of how many people could be standing on *your* shoulders to build something on top of what you have built, and think of the benefits you could derive from that. We believe that the old mantra of "let go and you will receive" will manifest itself here.

④ Myth 4. Musicians make music to make a lot of money.
This is one of the most astoundingly widespread misunderstandings about why musicians do what they do. The argument goes like this: "If we don't make even tougher laws that shore up, wall off, and extend copyright, and make all violations a serious crime, and go after those disgusting criminals who download our *product* without paying us . . . then our poor,

starving artists will not be motivated to crank out the goods any longer."
This is the equivalent of a pre–Civil War plantation owner alleging that
his slaves won't want to pick cotton anymore if there is a free market for
selling it.

Who actually believes that money is really what motivates musicians? The common contention that the music companies actually
represent the artists that they are so sweepingly and regularly refer-
ring to when commenting on this, is, in most cases, a far cry from the
truth. Ownership of the artist, or their intellectual property, may be a
better term to characterize the record label/artist relationship.

Musicians made a living making music long before there was
any way to record, productize, and build an industry on it. Yet the
industry now expects them to willingly accept being paid a pittance
in return for what amounts to, in most cases, indentured servi-
tude. Music has always been an ephemeral art, and the return was
not always measured in hard dollars. Musicians entertain people,
and derive benefits from that. In Mexico, for example, CD piracy is
rampant, and the industry is struggling, but still . . . plenty of music is
being performed, created, and sold, without any ties to the commercial recorded music sector, whatsoever. An entire culture of music
exists where musicians play concerts and special events, and where
their recordings are made and sold without their approval or financial involvement—much like the Grateful Dead in the '70s and '80s.
These musicians benefit strictly from the popularity that results from
their ubiquitous presence in the marketplace: higher admission
prices for concerts, larger venues, and larger sales of merchandise.

Ask musicians about their favorite parts of being in the business,
and the majority will say they like playing live shows. Musicians,
writers, and composers do what they do for *personal* reasons (at
least, most of them do), not because they set out to make millions of
dollars and feel a burning need to feed the record business by delivering a finished CD by a certain deadline. If making a big profit was
their prime motivator or their real intention, yes, *then* you would see
95 percent of them dropping out or never trying it to begin with.

Big Music has it backwards: people make music because they are
emotionally and creatively driven to do so. They do it because they don't
really have a choice not to—it is simply what they do—not because they
are looking at potential profits or to protect some rights they may have.

Let's face it: the creation of most music comes from the bottom up, not from the top down. Musicians made music long before there ever was any record industry, and they will continue to make music after the industry as we know it has gone the way of the helium blimp. If an artist has a message, if someone is really moved by him or her, if something really unique happens when the artist performs, and if that performance touches people's lives, it *will* have rewards for that artist. And technology has always been the artist's friend, not his enemy.

This is why powerful middlemen and their bean counters and legal eagles have artificially but nevertheless skillfully propped up the definition of copyright. Most musicians know that they must give freely to take freely, and in that spirit, not everything they create can be owned, forever. The current copyright canon exists largely for the benefit of the artist's "masters"—the record company and the publisher.

5 Myth 5. It takes millions of dollars to successfully launch an artist's career.

The Faustian pact of musicians and the music business, that "you'll need millions from a major label" to succeed—this myth has been carefully cultivated so that the fear of God is put into artists who may want to set out on their own. Artists think, "There is no way I can do this without the label . . . they are asking for a lot, but I had better sign with them because otherwise I will be broke for the rest of my life . . . "

The other myth that goes along with this "big money myth" is the illusion of fame and glamour: that every musician needs to be in a major act that plays Madison Square Garden, has videos that air on MTV, and travels the world in a leased jet. Only handfuls of musicians get to live like this, and the odds are really stacked against anyone who tries.

These expectations have fuelled thousands of bands, and that has taken its toll on hundreds of thousands of aspiring musicians. What a distorted view of reality! For every musician who makes it to the top of the charts, there are thousands of others less famous who enjoy meaningful careers producing, teaching, gigging, and writing music, on a modest budget. The truth is that over three thousand new CDs enter the market every month, and only 3 percent of those ever sell more than five thousand copies. The chances of making it really big by signing with a major label are ridiculously low.

Many young and aspiring artists believe that getting a label deal is the only way they can become successful. This is absolutely not true, and more and more artists are starting to figure that out. The real truth is that you need to do it yourself—because you always had to, anyway.

How have artists had to do it themselves? Well, in order to get major label attention, artists need to possess certain qualities that are considered essential to their success. Many artists feel that they need to do all these things to impress the A&R guys, so that they can start their careers, not realizing that they themselves have already started their careers. Take a look at some of the quotes, straight from A&R people in the biz, explaining what they look for in a band:

> The one thing I always tell people when I'm asked or on panels, and it sounds flip, but it's 1,000 percent true, is: be amazing. If you are truly amazing, we will find you. There is no way U2, REM, Smashing Pumpkins, Josh Rouse, etc., etc. would not get signed. If you are doing something that stands out, you will get noticed—it doesn't matter if you're in NYC or in Bosnia. The net (pun intended) is spread so wide at this point that you can really be anywhere and get noticed.
>
> Once you're noticed, what closes the deal for me is if you have a good infrastructure and if I'm not starting from scratch. It's very hard to take a band from zero sales to 20k–50k. Ideally, the artist/band has a constituency and fan base and has maybe self-released a few records so they understand the business side a little. Basically, the more you bring to a label, the less the label can take from you.
>
> —George Howard, President, Rykodisc

> Nothing gets my attention faster than proven success. Many bands/artists show up with no experience at all. They are waiting for a record company to come along and make them famous. REAL artists/bands aren't waiting on anyone. They're out making noise. That's what makes me take a second look.
>
> —Dean Diehl, Reunion/Provident Music Group

Artists really don't need traditional record companies to become successful. Indeed, if you get one to sign you, you already have done the hard work. Why give it all up for lame contracts and a few dollars? Look at CD Baby (www.cdbaby.com): they are among the very few survivors from the music.com battlefields, but they represent some of the non-traditional ways to sell music and make a good living. CD Baby provides a very easy way for independent artists to sell their CDs and digital tracks online. Since their founding, they have paid out over $10 million to artists for sales of their music. Their founder, Derek Sivers, is the real deal, and he does a great job of openly communicating with the artist community.

The Future of Music Marketing and Promotion

Marketing is the "eight-hundred-pound gorilla" of the music business, but new technologies will catapult marketing into King Kong territory. Music marketing has always been, and will always be, about exposure and discovery. Without exposure, an artist's new music will not get heard, and without being discovered by new fans, an artist's career is at a standstill. But when the traditional exposure and discovery method hits the digital highway, it gets a thousand times faster, larger, and more competitive.

For the past seventy years or so, the major record labels have controlled marketing and distribution, along with their radio and retail partners. They have had 360 degrees of control on the music business, and their moguls achieved godlike status—witness MCA's Lew Wasserman and Hollywood's Sid Sheinberg. The vast majority of music sold has been mass-marketed and spoon-fed to us. The means of exposure were primarily radio airplay and MTV, and the prime methods of discovery were live shows, music retailers, MTV, magazines, word of mouth, and . . . listening to radio.

Today, we are exposed to new music in a myriad of new ways, both passively and actively. Traditional radio and television are quickly losing ground. According to a 2003 Yahoo research report, avid Internet surfers are watching 32 percent less television, and listening to radio has been all but banished from any environment other than the car. Music is programmed on Muzak broadcasts, on Sirius and XM satellite radio services, and is used more than ever before in commercials, films, games, software, and on television.

Most consumers want and need tastemakers or taste-agents, credible personalities and proven entities that package programs and expose us to new music. This is why word-of-mouth marketing works so well. It builds on the trust of friends to propel a new song into the public consciousness. A friend is a true tastemaker.

We tend to be open to new music that is similar or at least related to music we already like. The artist is often the stepping-stone to discovery. People prefer to listen to new songs from artists who they already know, or who are closely related or endorsed by the ones they already know. This is confirmed in many studies of user behavior patterns in online radio. Online radio listeners program their channels based on artists they are already familiar with. Familiarity anchors the listener in a comfortable space; from there, he can step out to explore new music.

Fortunately for all of us, the days of one-size-fits-all mass marketing and global superstars for a global audience are quickly coming to an end. In the very near future, distribution—and even more importantly, marketing—will shift towards digital means. Ultimately, marketing will *be* distribution. Consumers already have far more choices of where to find and buy music, and what format to accept it in, whether they are renting, owning, or "borrowing." Digitally empowered music fans are some of the new tastemakers, and they are going to drive the business.

So where is the future of music marketing headed? New, integrated, direct, and personalized methods of exposure and discovery are taking shape all around us. Traditional radio is losing steam while digital/ online, cable, and satellite radio hold great promise. Promotion of new music in commercials, like U2's "Vertigo" iPod ad, and via a vast variety of sponsorship options, is gaining ground. Opportunities to break new artists online and through direct product tie-ins are rapidly expanding as the worlds of fashion and design, branding, games, movies, DVDs, and music intermingle. For example, Tony Hawk video games bring new artists and skateboarding maniacs together, uniting them in ways that put incredible power into the hands of a savvy marketer.

Technology is changing the way music is marketed almost as fast as it is changing the way music is distributed. We are starting to discover new music through many non-traditional means, including video games, in toys, on DVD, on our cell phones, and on the Web. Wireless networks promise to radically transform the music business once again. Music and its marketing is going mobile in a wide variety of ways.

Traditional Radio: The Death of the DJ

For many years, radio was the dominant method of exposing new music to the fans. It worked well because it was ubiquitous, free, and without a whole lot of competition. Radio was a terrific source of news, traffic and weather reports, and music—in the car, at work, and at home. It is a passive and non-interactive form of entertainment, because it does not dominate our attention in quite the same way that television, reading, and surfing the Web do.

The symbiotic relationship between radio stations, DJs, promoters, and record labels has been well documented. Most notorious in this relationship is the common practice of "buying" airtime for new records. In the past, many well-financed labels used independent promoters to encourage program directors to play their songs. An enormous amount of money and other forms of persuasion, including vacations, cars, drugs, and assorted "intangible benefits" have been used to grease the wheels of music commerce. Radio DJ Alan Freed called these payments "consulting fees," and many labels, small and large, used them to break records on the air. But the consolidation of radio ownership has made this under-the-table method of promotion less and less effective, as playlists homogenize and synchronize with the interests of radio's new corporate owners.

In 1996, the Telecommunications Act was passed, in an effort to pursue the "core public interest concerns of promoting diversity and competition." It eliminated the established cap on radio station ownership and increased the number of stations that any single entity could own in a given market. This, in effect, resulted in the formation of several parent companies that came to dominate the radio market—in our opinion, putting a cultural lock on the regional markets for music, and actually making the radio market less diverse, instead of more diverse. This development greatly benefited media conglomerates such as Infinity Broadcasting and Clear Channel Communications. Clear Channel, based in San Antonio, Texas owns more than twelve hundred radio stations in 99 percent of the 250 largest markets. Clear Channel also owns at least 130 concert venues, arenas, theaters, and nightclubs, as well as hundreds of thousands of billboards and outdoor advertising properties.

Clear Channel is a huge force in the entertainment industry, and its power continues to grow as it adds essential pieces of the puzzle to its core radio, live entertainment, and advertising base. The company recently acquired a crucial patent on recording live shows and now claims that it has the exclusive patent on selling live recordings immediately after the conclusion of a live show. Clear Channel has also begun to provide seed capital for new artists with a broad view towards artist management, publishing, touring, and other activities.

The consolidation of radio station ownership since 1996 has resulted in a disturbing homogeneity so profound that you can hear the same songs in nearly every market as you drive across the U.S. The songs at the top of the playlists get played over and over again within their formats. Playlists are "shared" between stations, and much of the programming is done on a centralized, national level, with many stations acting as automated satellite operations to corporate programming.

The Berklee Media division of Berklee College of Music conducted a study in June 2004 of radio airplay patterns across Contemporary Hit Radio (CHR)/Rhythmic, Country, Urban, and CHR/Pop formats in multiple cities in the U.S. The study showed that the biggest stations in the biggest markets were playing the same songs an average of 58 percent of the time. When station ownership was taken into account, the five CHR/Pop stations owned by Clear Channel were playing the same songs an average of 73 percent of the time. Apparently, it is profitable to limit the choices of new music available to the mass market.

Clear Channel is so powerful—reaching one-third of the U.S. population—that unless record companies can get a song played on their stations, they don't have much of a chance of breaking new music via radio. The consolidation of control and programming across the industry has made it nearly impossible for independent artists to get any relevant radio airplay whatsoever, and in our opinion, it is one of the many reasons that the record industry is in such trouble.

While independent radio stations programmed by local program directors still exist (such as college radio and rare gems like KCRW in Santa Monica), the largest stations in the biggest markets are controlled by corporate entities seeking to maximize their advertising revenues. Programmers pick songs and calculate playlists that provide maximum time for advertising and other sources of revenue. The role of the DJ has been relegated to announcing songs in many cases. In addition, the payola practices of the old days have been morphed into legitimized "promotional payments" where stations can essentially charge to "add" a song to their playlists, as part of purchasing promotion and marketing programs from the station.

These practices, and the lack of regionally or individually controlled radio programming, have made traditional radio a far less effective means of marketing new music, for all but the very few who can afford it. Discovering new music is certainly not what commercial radio in the U.S. is about, today. By and large, that process has now moved to the Internet and the multitude of file-sharing services and on-demand online radio stations.

In 2002, radio listening hit a twenty-seven–year low, and station owners have been hard pressed for new ideas and ways of recapturing the market. Already, television, video games, cell phones, and Internet usage have taken a big chunk out of the time that people listen to radio. As the record labels struggle to maintain their footing in the digital marketplace, traditional radio stations are beginning to realize that their lunch is also just about to be swallowed up in the seismic shift towards the digital distribution and marketing of music.

Internet Radio and Podcasting: The Infinite Array of Choices

Despite witnessing the most consolidated and homogenized traditional radio environment ever, we are also looking at a steady rise in the number of alternate services. Of these new music broadcast alternatives, online radio has become the most prevalent. Radio airplay over the Internet—Webcasting—reaches increasingly large audiences around the world and provides listeners with the truly diverse music programming that they are looking for.

There are countless Internet radio service providers today. AOL, Musicmatch, and Yahoo's Launch dominate the Internet Broadcasting Arbitron Ratings. AOL's Internet Radio Network is the most widely listened to, with an estimated four million unique listeners who tune in at least once a month. The AOL network includes Radio@AOL, Radio@Netscape, Spinner, Winamp, and SHOUTcast.

Many of these services allow users to customize their listening experience, and therefore offer some added values. The Musicmatch Internet radio network's most popular channel is the Musicmatch ArtistMatch service. With ArtistMatch, users select their favorite artists, and the system programs the channel with those and other related artists, much like Amazon offers book recommendations to its customers upon login. Among the other most widely used Internet radio networks at the time of this writing are Launch, MSN Radio,

Radiopass, Virgin Radio, ABC Radio Network, NPR, CBC, Educational Media Foundation, KillerOldies.com, and Live365.com. This list is bound to grow very dramatically once Internet radio can increase the quality of its streams.

Internet radio is a terrific way for new music to get exposed and associated with particular genres, related artists, and tastemakers. Music programmers at these Internet radio stations serve up an increasingly wide variety of new music from indie labels and individual artists, as well as by all of the majors. This source of content programming is a great vein for music marketers to tap and can provide exposure for their artists in an environment that supports creative discovery and diverse tastes.

Perhaps even more interesting is the Podcasting phenomenon, for which we have the former MTV VJ Adam Curry to thank. A Podcast is a very clever way to deliver MP3 audio via the 'Net as a simple subscription feed that can be automatically delivered to iTunes and your iPod, or other MP3 players for listening whenever you want. Podcasting began in mid 2004 and will have spread like wildfire by the time you read this. Like text-based news that can be aggregated in an RSS news reader, Podcasts deliver personalized radio at little or no cost to either the Podcasters of the listeners. Podcasting is pirate radio for the twenty-first century, and will have as profound an effect on traditional radio as blogging has had on publishing.

Satellite Radio: The Return of the DJ

Two competing services already deliver near-CD-quality digital music directly to your car, home, or office via satellite. XM Radio and Sirius offer a wide variety of music choices that cater to nearly every niche imaginable, and most are commercial-free. Satellite radio receivers display the name of the song and artist playing, making it easy to discover and find out about something new. Users may also browse through their selected stations in a variety of ways. You may have noticed the odd little antennae down the back or top of some cars; at the time of this writing, nearly three million satellite radio receivers have been installed in the United States.

Satellite radio broadcasters start to resemble the heyday of traditional music radio, when the personality and vision of the DJs were important parts of the listening experience. These digital DJs offer hope for a broadcast format that can blend the best of traditional radio with new modes of digital discovery and interactivity. As these new satellite services mature and grow in popularity, they will become an increasingly important vehicle for fans who delight in the discovery of music.

Music Television: What a Lovely Ride It Was

In 1982, MTV arrived on the music scene and quickly became the most powerful "radio" station on the planet. With a direct reach into the households of literally tens of millions of young music fans, MTV almost single-handedly transformed the business of music marketing by packaging artists for delivery via television. MTV meant that in order to break a band, you needed a killer video. Video budgets began to vastly outstrip recording budgets, and the way an artist looked and acted on the small screen became seemingly more important than how they sounded. The single became more important than the album, and some people would say that music became more about marketing than the music, itself. Michael Jackson became an unprecedented global star in no small part due to the videos of *Thriller*, a record that became the greatest selling album in history (until topped by the Eagles). The same was true for Madonna, Eminem, Britney Spears, and many others. MTV drove the music business to focus on videos, and artists were given their three minutes onscreen to either make it big or be tossed aside. Therefore, MTV also became the means for record labels to quickly identify the hit artists that they would continue to promote and develop.

But over time, and much like radio, music television programming became less and less diverse and more and more expensive for the labels, to the point that it was no longer very effective in representing the cutting edge. It had simply become part of the establishment. MTV had begun to pick and choose the videos that they would play, and in so doing, became somewhat of a gatekeeper of popular culture. Now, however, MTV has been forced to bend to advertising concerns and has changed its entire format, dropping music videos from a majority of its programming slots, and developing new show formats like *The Osbournes* to maintain or increase audience share.

This game is clearly changing, and in countries such as Germany, other television music services such as VIVA have already put a big dent into MTV's world domination plans. Maybe diversification always follows homogenization . . .

Over the last twenty years, music channels like MTV, VH1, and BET have come to be used as a primary major-label promotion strategy. Channels like MTV could make and break artists. The problem with MTV is that it mostly plays to its most responsive sector of the market—teenagers. Thus, we expect to see Justin Timberlake et al when we tune in to MTV, while the vast majority of the music-loving public has to go to their CD players or the Internet to tap into something they actually enjoy.

Sponsorship: The Lure of Cool

Music has been marketed via product tie-ins, to a degree, for many years, but sponsorships have increasingly been used to introduce new music and services to the public. With the inherent challenges in traditional music marketing via radio, labels have turned to product associations and the placement of songs in film, video, and television programming. If you have watched movies or network television over the past ten years, you certainly have noticed that song placement in advertisements and in popular television shows like *The OC* is a powerful means of exposing new artists to the marketplace.

Celine Dion's big break came when she sang the title song to Disney's *Beauty and the Beast*. A&M Records got a major boost when Jaguar used Sting's "Desert Rose" in a car commercial. When the British band Dirty Vegas got "Days Go By" placed in a television commercial for the Mitsubishi Eclipse, the exposure helped it nab a Grammy nomination for Best Dance Recording. Jet got a boost when "Are You Gonna Be My Girl" powered some of the first iPod television ads. Labels are targeting particular demographics by using music from artists and songs most likely to appeal. The hit show, product, or movie then becomes the tastemaker, and the songs grow popular by association.

Sometimes this works in reverse, as stated by Mitsubishi Motors President and CEO Pierre Gagnon on MSNBC (2001):

The most powerful proof is when a DJ comes onto the radio and says, "And now, the Mitsubishi song." It's hard to explain the phenomenon. What we're so pleased with is we know we're breaking through when these songs become more popular.

The music industry is now actively courting major corporations for partnerships and marketing tie-ins, holding its first ever "upfront" conference in September 2004, according to *Rolling Stone.* The showcase was designed to pitch hot bands to hot companies and products like Mercedes-Benz and Pepsi. "Target your brands with our bands" was the mantra.

There are many other, more subtle ways of promoting music via product tie-ins. Look at the custom CD compilations created by Starbucks to see a product tie-in at work. Or consider the New Age CDs being sold in health-food stores. All around us are opportunities for music to be associated with a product or lifestyle.

The year 2004 saw an incredible amount of digital music being marketed in association with mass-market products, beginning with the Super Bowl 2004 promotion deal between Pepsi and Apple Computer to give away one hundred million iTunes downloads. While this is not promotion of specific songs or artists, it is a promotion for legitimate digital downloading that had a huge impact on people's awareness of digital music. Similar collaborations are underway between the re-branded Napster (acquired out of bankruptcy by Roxio and turned into a "legitimate" digital music site) and name brands like Miller Beer and Energizer batteries, as well as between Sony Connect and marketing powerhouses McDonald's, United Airlines, and Intel. Bono and U2 are screaming in an iPod ad, promoting their new song "Vertigo" and a custom-branded black iPod itself! Interesting to note that U2 took no money for the ad appearance, instead opting for royalties on the iPod. Smart.

Coca-Cola created a digital downloading store in Great Britain at mycokemusic.com, and many more brands are following suit. Labels and artists wishing to associate themselves with the soft drink giant will have a great opportunity to test the waters there. Companies like Coke, Pepsi, Heineken, and Miller, which target young audiences, see a clear opportunity to use music and the "cool" factor of digital downloading to strengthen their customers' brand affinity. It is not a promotion of the drink itself that drives their customers to choose their brand; it is the association with the new music. Associating with lots of artists and genres will help them reach a wide audience and could be a real boost for emerging artists—and technology will power this process.

It remains to be seen if these sponsorships will ultimately prove to be fruitful for the record companies over the long term. Sponsorships seem like an easier way for latecomers into this space to try to break into an increasingly crowded legitimate digital music marketplace. Sure, leading consumer brands want to be associated with the cool and hip nature of music, but do artists and musicians necessarily want to be associated with those brands? Who is making these partnership choices, and what will the impact eventually be on people's behavior? How exactly are people being asked to pay for their music? While Jack Daniels and Jim Beam may seem likely partners for Lynyrd Skynyrd, it is hard to believe that pitches for "free" music from Pepsi, Sprite, Papa John's Pizza, 7-Eleven stores, Target, McDonald's, or the Energizer bunny are going to make people continue to want to pay for digital downloads when the freebies go away.

Direct Marketing: Knowing Your Customers

Most recorded music has been mass marketed from record labels to the fans. For the most part, the labels had no real idea who was purchasing their CDs and had no way of establishing a direct relationship between the fans and the artist or label.

Direct marketing, when properly done, is a way of establishing and building a direct relationship between the company producing the product or service, and its customers. This relationship is used to identify customers and profile their interests and needs so that the company can more effectively market its current and future products and services to them.

If music companies develop direct relationships with their customers, like fan clubs, they can deliver music directly to fans, can market merchandise, concert tickets, limited edition products, live recordings, fan clubs, access to artists, and other appealing products and services. Some of the best-positioned companies in this market-place of the future may very well be the concert promoters and venues. They have direct contact with the music fans and can therefore develop and mine the relationships that they can develop into the digital space.

Many labels are using new technology and new marketing techniques to their advantage, as they create new and exciting promotion tools. The majority of these new promotion tools use direct marketing techniques to create and maintain relationships with fans, fostering the loyalty that often comes with such relationships. Mailing lists keep fans updated on shows and events, while at the same time allowing for the band to get a better idea of the demographic of its fan base. Eminem and Prince have been able to fill almost half of the seats at large arenas with their fan clubs.

String Cheese Incident is an example of a band that created its own label and that uses free music offerings and direct marketing to build up a loyal fan base. The band started out with Usenet postings between the band and their fans, and they encouraged direct connections and trading of live tapes of their shows to build up a mailing list. The band's label SCI Fidelity now uses direct marketing methods and affinity programs to promote shows, taking the product and service metaphor to new heights by forming a network of eight different companies, including their own travel agency, to book blocks of rooms and sell them to fans who want to see the shows as the band travels around the country. The band provides tools that let their fans trade music online, participate in festivals, and network with like-minded fans around the country. The band now grosses over $1.5 million a year playing live gigs, and they can easily ship one hundred thousand units of each new album that they release to their fans. The SCI model is starting to work for other artists as well. The label now boasts eleven acts, including Keller Williams and Steve Winwood.

Without a doubt, the Internet is a very effective tool for marketing artists online and for developing lucrative relationships between artists and fans. The obvious examples are artist Web sites where music can be sampled and purchased, either as downloads or as physical CDs shipped to the fan. Merchandise can also be sold. The Web site can host a community of fans who can meet and chat with each other about the music and can serve as a terrific vehicle to build a mailing list and establish direct connections between artists and fans.

The Web provides an excellent platform for artists to more directly control their careers. Through direct marketing, artists and their management can direct their promotional efforts in ways that appeal to their fans, without having to depend on the overworked staff at their labels to do the entire job.

Artists can promote tours, shows, and concerts via the Web, and if the venue allows artists to directly book tickets, they can even sell tickets. This generally is not possible at large venues or via the major concert promoters, but tickets for smaller clubs and shows can often be sold online. At the very least, the shows can be promoted, and contests and other offers can be used to gather fans' names—with the grand prize being backstage passes or a chance to meet or talk with the artists.

Of course, the Internet is at its best when used to reach a targeted market niche. Once an artist has found an audience somewhere—through playing gigs, selling records at their shows, and gaining some grass-roots momentum, the 'Net can be used to target and increase this audience. Knowing the audience and then engaging them, encouraging them to recommend an artist to their friends, finding other artists like them, and expanding the relationships, all can lead to an engine that can propel careers forward, regardless of where the music is actually sold. But it can be a lot more rewarding for the artist if they sell directly.

Niche marketing allows labels to focus their efforts and approach on a smaller number of fans, and lets them hone their marketing messages to address the needs of a defined group of people. Labels offering a personalized approach and direct connection between the artist and the fan should consider link exchanges with other artists and labels in similar genres. Tell-a-friend sign-ups offer incentives to register for site membership or mailing lists. Or pay-for-access music subscription sites, which include live chats with artists, backstage passes, priority tickets, personalized merchandise, clothing, posters, games, and samples from forthcoming albums, create entirely new experiences for music fans and strong relationships between the company and their customers.

Video Games: Targeting Players with New Music

The video game industry generated $28 billion in revenue in 2002 and is arguably one of the most significant sources of entertainment today. It is a sensational phenomenon, particularly among young boys, who make up a voracious market for new music, and who already spend more time playing video games than listening to radio. When Electronic Arts ships their new "Madden" football video game, each song on the game will receive over seven hundred million spins in the first six months. That is an incredible number of impressions, and it delivers new music to young fans in entirely new ways. Compare the number of spins per song on the game with potential radio spins, and you see that these songs are being heard on video games more than the no. 1 record in America is being heard on radio over the same time period. This is a very significant shift in how new music is discovered.

Steve Schnur, Worldwide Executive of Music and Audio for Electronic Arts, describes how EA capitalizes on the video game phenomenon to introduce new music to willing fans:

> An unsigned band, Avenged Sevenfold, was launched in Madden NFL 2004. They had the right management, were on the Warped Tour, and then launched in Madden. In the first week of Madden's release, their CD sold more than five thousand units. MTV took notice. The touring and video game exposure helped the band to sell thousands of CDs—and to get signed to both EMI Publishing and Warner Bros. Records.
>
> Blink-182, a massive international band, also debuted a single, "Feeling This," in Madden NFL 2004. The song didn't even go to radio until two months after the game release. Radio stations received so many calls that the song started to get played right off of the video game and soon charted. Over the past two years, stars like Outkast, Radiohead, Franz Ferdinand, Green Day, the Hives, Fatboy Slim, Snoop Dog, Xzibit, Chingy, Chevelle, Black Eyed Peas, Christina Aguilera, Busta Rhymes, Kings of Leon, the Roots, Queens of the Stone Age, the Red Hot Chili Peppers, DMX, Sum 41, Nelly, the Crystal Method, Jimmy Eat World, Jane's Addiction, the Donnas, and literally hundreds more have become an enthusiastic part of EA games.

"Feeling This" went on to become Blink-182's bestseller. Clearly, the hugely popular video and computer gaming platforms represent significant opportunities for labels and artists to gain massive exposure. Watch for "Def Jam Fight for New York," a new game set for release by EA at the time of this writing. While not available to all bands, this is a pointer towards a very successful form of music marketing that does not depend in any way on radio airplay or MTV. As more and more television, gaming, and online channels are developed, music can ride their popularity to new heights of exposure. Electronic Arts has become a gatekeeper and tastemaker for new music.

Cell Phones and Wireless: Direct Marketing on Steroids

People are more reliant on their cell phones than ever before, and the dependence is growing. People can now surf the 'Net using only their cell phones, and they can participate in a wide range of activities, such as checking e-mail, text messaging, sports scores, and stock quotes, getting ring tones, and sending pictures to other phones. Online communication is no longer the exclusive domain of computers; a vast network of information and communication is becoming available to anyone who has a mobile phone.

Cross an iPod with a cell phone and you have a networked mobile music player. Nokia has introduced a similar product—a cell phone that can also play video games. Apple and Motorola announced that Motorola will begin shipping lots of cell phones incorporating iTunes technology in early 2005. Expect to see a virtual explosion in networked audio players in the next few years.

In 2003, ring tones made up a nearly $3.5-billion-dollar business and are projected to grow to $6–7 billion by 2008, a clear indication of what can happen when it becomes easy for people to download legitimate digital music. More interesting is the fact that people seem willing to pay a lot more money for a ten-second sound sample than they would to download an entire track; companies charge $1.99 to $2.50 for each ring tone purchased. That is a lot more money than the record companies are getting for a complete digital track on iTunes, Napster, or Rhapsody. Convenience and ease of use wins again.

We believe that this behavior resonates so well with the cellular customer because they are enjoying a pure form of entertainment through customizing their phone. It provides an association and identity for that person. This $3.5 billion dollars in a few years is a huge business—but that's what can happen when music is marketed as a form of entertainment. *Music is entertainment*—and when packaged and promoted as such, it sells like hotcakes. Look for the wireless carriers to begin to promote these features heavily around the world. Ring tones leap over one of the biggest barriers facing consumers in the digital marketplace: that of easy payment. People already pay a monthly bill for the phone service, so a few extra dollars for custom content is very easy for people to deal with.

Ring tones represent another vehicle for artists to reach their audience, and that may have massive implications for the future. Motorola is partnering with well-known club DJ/producers and MTV to promote new music to cell phone users. Paul van Dyk, Felix da Housecat, and DJ Colette are some of the DJs creating new music for ring-tone distribution. Motorola has developed MotoMixer software (www.hellomoto.com), which lets its cell phone customers actually remix the DJ-produced ring tones, creating a kind of collaboration platform between artists and fans. Quoted in a recent *Billboard* article, Motorola's Rob Gelick, manager of entertainment content, says, "We're offering a more engaging listening experience—one that allows for more self-expression. Albums still make sense for artistic reasons, but ring tones have the potential to become the new single."

Cell phones are now being used to promote artists and bands around the world. Using a combination of text messaging and picture transportation, cell phone owners receive information like tour dates, album releases, special events, and songs. In Japan and in other Asian countries, cell phones have become the major source of entertainment and information, delivering music, news, sports, and everything else people want. In Japan, concerts are routinely promoted via cell phones. Fans can purchase tickets and select seats from their cell phone screen and keypad. The phones are even used as the ticket machines, admitting the fan into the venue via a code on the cell phone.

Internet radio is also getting into the cell phone marketing game. A partnership between Webcaster Radiostorm.com and network operator StreamGuys makes it possible to listen to Internet radio streams on your cell phone. Using the browser on a wireless-enabled cell phone, fans can select from a list of available stations and have commercial-free music streamed directly to their cell phone. With the appropriate adapter, fans can then listen to customized Internet radio broadcasts in their cars as they drive to and from work each day.

Once the SMS-support technologies finally arrive in the U.S., it will be time for artists and promoters to jump on the bandwagon, as they have already done in Europe and Asia. (SMS stands for short messaging service.) With permission-based mobile media, marketers can send messages directly to the palm (or ears) of cell phone users. Studies in Europe show this to be a much more effective method of advertising than television or radio, or even e-mail.

Wireless networks are going to completely transform the marketing and delivery of music in the future. Internet hotspots, Web-enabled cell phones, handheld computers, portable video-game players, and of course the establishment of a much more realistic and efficient content licensing scheme will converge to create a seamless experience—*music like water*. It is as exciting and transforming as the development of the transistor radio, which sparked a technological revolution that propelled the music industry and drove listener behavior and revenues to unprecedented levels.

Marketing Lessons from an Unlikely Source

The music industry can learn a lot by looking at other businesses that have been affected drastically by technology. One such business is pornography, and the transformation that it went through during the past twenty years. It has been said that in the early days of the Internet, the number-one activity was looking for and surfing on porn sites. This is probably still true today, though for a short period around 1999, the number-one word most used in Web-based search engines changed from "sex" to "MP3." Early online porn businesses, most of them entirely new, drove the expansion of the World Wide Web and largely defined e-commerce as we know it today. The people and companies that were dominant in the porn industry at the birth of the Web are no longer dominant. Literally thousands of new businesses are thriving, and the game has changed dramatically. Musicians, entrepreneurs, and savvy record labels should pay very close attention.

Prior to 1980, the porn business was largely the domain of magazine publishers offering pornographic images and stories, and filmmakers delivering both soft- and hard-core products. In the early 1980s, the discovery of AIDS and the fear that resulted as people began to question their attitudes toward sex, made it possible for porn to take a major leap forward, appearing as a safe-sex alternative. The timing was also such that the television, videocassette recorder, and telephone were available as platforms for new forms of pornography to ride on—and ride, they did.

The adult video industry began to produce new video products for distribution via mail order and in sex shops, and the phone-sex industry exploded. In both of these cases, the business people who really benefited by the growth and establishment of these new products and services were not the established porn players at the time, but new "independent" purveyors who grew to become dominant in their niches.

Just as porn was a primary driver for the adoption of the VHS cassette as the preferred video format, porn has also played a major role in establishing e-commerce on the Web and in driving online business models. The online porn business was responsible for the sale of lots of routers, servers, and other Internet infrastructure equipment in the '90s. There is a voracious appetite for pornography. The entire industry was changed from one of primarily publishing products, to a vast network of vendors and businesses producing products and services, many of them new, borne of the new medium. Again, the primary beneficiaries of this expansion were the new entrepreneurs—and of course, the customers.

The big magazine brands of that time, including *Playboy*, *Penthouse*, and *Hustler*, established their own porn sites. At first, these were online versions of the magazines, using their archives. These sites drew significant traffic, although not much in the way of revenue or profits. The Internet was different. As these powerhouses soon found out, the 'Net eliminated a huge barrier to entry, namely the cost of printing and distributing a national or international magazine. Very soon, new competitors were able to establish major traffic in pornography and lucrative revenue streams. Early adult Web sites were able to attract very significant customer bases. These businesses, unencumbered by an existing publishing operation and having less to lose, were able to better exploit the opportunities that the Web affords.

The magazines looked at their business as selling a "product" and treated online porn in the same way. When they first moved online, the magazines were not especially nimble and did not foresee the multitude of product and service opportunities that others did. They also had a difficult time competing with the free porn that began to appear everywhere, and a lot of this free stuff consisted of pirated images, scanned and stolen from the big magazines themselves. They were forced to police the 'Net themselves and try to contain the piracy via litigation and closing down Web sites. Before too long, there was a critical mass of free product well beyond that pirated from the magazines, and the game was changed. Does this sound familiar?

The Web made it possible for new independent porn businesses to flourish, increasing overall revenue some ten-fold, according to some estimates. It opened up opportunities for entirely new entrepreneurs who saw the potential of the medium and established multiple sources of revenue. This was especially true for niche sites that could bring targeted content online, and it almost immediately began generating revenue. This was also true for some of the established models and video porn stars, who were able to parlay their name recognition into a URL to drive Internet traffic to their personal Web sites.

Today, online porn offers a rich variety of safe-sex alternatives, offering up every imaginable form of pornography, while maintaining users' anonymity, relatively speaking. In addition to collections and galleries of photographs and images offered up in the magazines, the Web sites offer movies, live chats with nude models, Webcams, live strippers, two-way video and audio conferencing, and more. Forever gone are the days of this business being controlled by a few powerful moguls like Hefner, Guccione, and Flynt. Anyone can become a pornographer online. Many did, and they have made a fortune doing so.

Now, what can we learn from porn, and how might it apply to the music business? For one, we believe that the online music business will follow the same pattern that the online porn business did, in the sense that the Internet will break the monopoly on distribution of music that the major labels have enjoyed since the invention of the phonograph. The major recorded music labels first established their own branded Web sites to promote their new releases, in much the same way that *Playboy* et al established their first sites as extensions of the magazines. Both the entrenched porn kings and the music kings failed to see the potential of the Internet for new business models, and were caught entirely off guard by what happened. Indeed, *Penthouse* magazine filed for bankruptcy protection in 2003, claiming that it had lost two thirds of its readership. They are not faring any better online. Playboy.com reportedly lost over $50 million in 2000 and 2001.

Just as happened to the porn business, and much to their horror, the major record labels found that a staggering amount of "free" music was available online and most of it was theirs. Napster gained incredible popularity in 1999, and very shortly thereafter, P2P networks caught fire and began to run rampant. Free music, like free porn, turns out to be very appealing to people. In response, the major labels launched Pressplay, Musicnet, and a few other "legitimate" Web sites to try to establish an online "product" that they could control. However, people did not want to play the game that way, and these sites never gained any traction. The majors were shown more clearly than ever that the brands that people were searching for were the artist brands, not the labels.

To better understand the future of music marketing offline, let's take a look at how the online porn sites established and promoted themselves. The entrepreneurs of the new online porn in the 1990s were faced with many of the same problems that face independent artists and new music today. How do you break through the clutter and get people to know about you? Playboy.com got lots of traffic initially because of the brand and the archive. But ultimately, they could not really compete with the torrent of new sites and the "free" sites, and did not get the large market share of the online business that they enjoyed in print. Others did, though, so how did they do it?

Online porn growth was driven by the search engines Yahoo, Altavista, and others that provided pointers to porn Web sites containing key words such as "sex." Once you got to many of these sites, you were exposed not only to the porn you were looking for, but also to a vast array of links to other, associated porn sites. The industry propelled the fortunes of the early online porn Webmasters by banding together to use the Web's hyperlinking capabilities. Some of the largest sites are actually elaborate networks of niche-market sites joined together to trade traffic. This collective behavior was perhaps the most important marketing tool that the porn Webmasters had at their disposal. Adult sites formed very large circles of sites, all linked to one another to boost the popularity of their links and their rankings on the search engines. If musicians today could execute on this strategy, they could usurp the power of radio and the major labels, once and for all.

Web linking created a vast network of adult Web sites that fed off each other's traffic to grow the entire industry. Indeed, this network approach spawned many of the software tracking and banner advertising technologies, such as pop-ups, that are widely used on the Web. This linking approach also was one of the first, albeit crude, examples of recommendation technologies, suggesting to users, "if you like this site, you might like these other sites."

There are thousands of Web sites that provide links to other porn sites. Sites dedicated to reviewing adult Web sites directed interested traffic to thousands of online porn sites. Entire networks of sites were formed, some within the control of a single entity and others across a collection of independent operators to drive traffic to each other's sites. Whether intentionally or out of necessity, the nascent industry worked as an online cooperative to promote and establish itself, and expand its influence a thousandfold over the former incumbent moguls of porn, mostly just by using free pix and lots-o-links.

Today, musicians may want to follow their lead and begin to emulate the linking, recommendation, collaborative filtering, and promotion engines. Independent labels could link to each other and to all of the individual artists' Web sites. Artists link to other artists, managers, agencies, and labels. Online directories of musicians and new releases offering reviews and samples can develop. But they must provide a fast and easy way to sample the songs, just as the porn sites provided thumbnail images to let you quickly scan their offerings. The browse capabilities found on the P2P networks are an attempt at this, as is the browsing and 30-second previewing found on the new Apple iTunes software.

One challenge will be to avoid creating another monolithic wasteland of unsigned bands such as the one found on MP3.com, and to embrace the Web for one of its strengths: the linking of apparently random things into some kind of order. Another challenge will be to make this order-out-of-chaos technology truly useful beyond the filtering that has been in use for music for many years now, including the original "Firefly" music recommendation software and the recommendations found on Amazon.

Musicians today do have P2P networks as very efficient means of distributing songs, albeit for free. The purveyors of online porn did not have P2P networks at their disposal to distribute and promote their sites and products. Indeed, these networks would probably not have worked very well as a promotion and distribution vehicle for online porn, since the current P2P networks are mostly designed to find content that you already know about. They may help you find pictures of Marilyn Monroe, but will not help you turn on the vast flood of porn that we have now.

P2P file-sharing of music became so popular because people already knew what to look for before they logged on. As such, Napster, Kazaa, and the whole P2P phenomenon pose the greatest threat to existing, well-known artists and songs from major labels, while they offer opportunity to new artists. New artists can use the networks to distribute their songs, but first they have to become known, and this still means facing the same old promotion problems that plague CD-based delivery. So, what kind of impact can the P2P and other distribution networks really have on the promotion of songs in the future?

P2P networks have already begun to exploit the linking and referral capability of the 'Net by allowing you to chat with other people online, and to peruse the collections of songs in the libraries of the people you are sharing files with. You may log onto the network to find the latest Pearl Jam tune, but then discover some vintage Neil Young in the folder along with Pearl Jam and fifty-six other bands. These features are only in their infant stages and are not particularly obvious or easy to use. However, with the Apple iTunes service, you can actually listen to tracks from other people on the same IP network quite easily, using their Rendezvous technology. This is one way to find new music that you might like, but you will have to actively look for it. The information won't come to you.

A big win for P2P networks will be when they start to harness the power of collaboration and recommendation, and begin to provide legal opportunities for new artists and labels to push out new songs to members of the network. There is already a move in this direction by Altnet and their partnership with Kazaa. Altnet provides a "pay for placement" opportunity for artists to promote their music on the Kazaa interface. This is not unlike the "slotting fees" charged by retailers or radio. This could be a huge growth area for these networks, if they can take on the task of promotion and create the next-generation music commerce machine. When the networks finally get this right, it will become the juggernaut that breaks the back of radio promotion as we know it today.

The porn business developed from a business model that derived revenues from commission-based link exchanges between sites in the early days, to a much more sophisticated combination of revenue streams, including subscriptions, pay-per-view, and offline sales such as DVDs. Exact revenue numbers are not known, but the online porn business is estimated to be a multi-billion-dollar industry, with the largest companies grossing several million dollars a month. Today's larger porn sites offer multiple subscription or membership options, including free trial periods (in exchange for an e-mail address), as well as monthly, three-month, six-month, and annual terms. Most sites still rely on revenues from advertising and link exchanges and networks to keep driving traffic. Many lead the customer down a path that includes offers for premium content, interaction with the models through exclusive private areas, live chats, Webcams, clubs, and other items for sale.

The sites rely on online promotion through link exchanges, click-through advertising, networks, and occasionally, some offline means of promotion. One of the main advantages offered by the 'Net is the direct contact that the sites have with their customers via e-mail. This is an extremely cost-effective means of promotion. Once you have developed an opt-in list of ready consumers, you can reach them again and again, for next to nothing.

"Free" continues to be a huge source of traffic and creates demand for online porn. Sites will almost always offer some sample images and sometimes movies from their archives, to get you "hooked," and an elaborate network of free sites and link pages usually lead the viewer to the paid content. It goes without saying that online porn sites would not exist if they had not and would not continue to give away a cornucopia of free content. This is a proven fact that musicians and labels must really pay attention to going forward. It represents a tremendous opportunity to develop direct contact between the musicians and the fans, through the trade of free content in return for an ongoing relationship. This is going to be a very potent way to market music.

Technology has completely transformed the porn business and the way that customers acquire the products or services. It is time to rethink the models for doing business between musicians and fans, in order to take advantage of the relationships that can be formed. Niche marketing will certainly become a dominant way for musicians to reach their audiences, in much the same way that porn reaches its audiences.

The Future of Music
Distribution and Acquisition

The recorded music industry is undergoing a radical change that will bring about a redefinition of the music business. The labels' single-bullet theory pins the blame for declining sales squarely on their disloyal customers and their use of file-trading networks such as the original Napster, and P2P services and sites such as Kazaa, Morpheus, Bearshare, iMesh, eDonkey, and others. The industry cites numerous studies that show the detrimental effects of illegal file-trading on revenue and profits.

But is file-sharing really to blame for the dismal downturn in CD sales? Evidence abounds that it is not. We believe that that argument is a convenient fig leaf for the industry to hide behind, rather than facing reality and accepting that the current business model is no longer going to work.

The Demise of the CD

We believe that the reasons for the decline in CD sales have very little to do with illegal file-sharing, and a great deal more to do with the way that music has been marketed and distributed for the past eight to ten years. These reasons include the significantly reduced number of retail outlets that carry CDs, the by-and-large non-competitive pricing of CDs and digital singles, the labels' unwillingness to experiment and develop really different artists, and the many competing forms of entertainment that exert magnetic power over the disposable dollars of the consumers, including video games, wireless services, and DVDs. And, let's not forget to mention that we have finally reached the end of that glorious replacement cycle of vinyl-to-CD that the industry has happily gorged itself on for the past fifteen to twenty years. Add to that the music fans' increasing awareness of the unfair way that record companies have treated artists, and you have some very good reasons as to why sales are down.

Competition from Other Media

Given most people's limited number of discretionary dollars available for entertainment, it is no wonder that sales of audio CDs have fallen dramatically. According to *Fortune* magazine, "Video games aren't just eating into entertainment dollars; they're taking up increasingly more of the *time* Americans once spent listening to music or at the movies." This phenomenon is not lost on companies like Electronic Arts (EA), which is incorporating new music and cinema-like experiences into the games themselves. The result: EA's stock has soared, despite all of Nasdaq's downward journeys.

There are now many more compelling entertainment alternatives, including video games, online porn, dating, network services, DVDs, and all kinds of software. These alternatives are usually more expensive than the CD, but deliver a tremendous relative value to the customer where the CD falls short—at least in terms of perception, which is ultimately how people make buying decisions. Compare the fifteen levels of exploration and entertainment value inherent in a modern video game like Kingdom Hearts or Tony Hawk, or the rich and engaging multiplayer environments available in a game such as Everquest, and you can clearly see that the CD simply no longer seems to be in the same league in terms of customers' value perceptions.

The End of the Replacement Cycle

Fewer people are purchasing CDs not because they can get the music for free, but because they are simply spending their money elsewhere. Therefore, it should be no surprise to the record companies that young music fans are turning to file-sharing instead of spending their limited allowance funds on something that just doesn't seem worth the money, when compared to what else is available. The bottom line: customers do what they think is right for themselves, and no amount of arm-wrestling or heavy-handed litigation is going to convince them otherwise. The only thing that works is *added value.*

CDs were developed to replace vinyl with a better quality, more portable, and more durable product. When CDs came onto the market and everyone had to convert from vinyl to digital, it was an unprecedented boom time for the music industry. Though that boom was unsustainable over the long term, everyone enjoyed it, and many a record executive grew fat and complacent. No wonder: just crank out the old stuff again, repackage it nicely, and rake in another huge round of cash. This resulted in cementing drastic, unrealistic expectations in regards to future revenues. However, after almost twenty years, today the CD replacement cycle has ended.

Yes, almost everyone did buy the same album twice. Why should the record companies expect that sales levels would remain the same or continue to increase?

Piracy and the Lack of New Formats

The RIAA has consistently equated the activity of the file-sharing public with that of the wholesale CD pirates who illegally manufacture CDs in mass quantities and distribute them through black-market channels. Wholesale, commercially organized CD piracy, most notably in China and Eastern Europe, may never be stopped completely but is something completely different in nature than P2P file-sharing.

However, while piracy of video games is rampant, as well, it really has not hurt the industry or threatened its existence. The same can also be said for the personal computer software market (with 57 percent average piracy, yearly) and the video market overall. The main reason that piracy has not negatively impacted the video game, video, or PC software businesses—and may actually have enhanced sales—is that the producers and developers are constantly reinventing their products. New game platforms (Playstation 1 and 2) come to market every couple of years and drive a completely new generation of game software products. Similarly, the software products themselves are regularly updated from V1.0 to V2.0 and so on, and video game makers quickly learned to update their products. Madden 2000 is not very appealing to gamers in 2004, and anyone trying to sell illegal copies most always plays catch-up with the legal versions.

The VHS tape was once considered Enemy #1 of the film industry, with MPAA boss Jack Valenti rallying against it whenever possible. "The VCR is to the American film producer and the American public as the Boston Strangler is to a woman alone," Valenti said in 1992. The industry attempted to block sales of video recorders because, they argued, it would kill the movie business. After a lot of quarreling and legal wrangling, the studios were not successful in stopping the march of technology. Today the film and video business is many times larger than it was when the VHS recorder was released. The videotape format actually grew the film/video business. Today, more people go to the movie theater than ever before.

The VHS actually became *another* way to enjoy a movie, not the only way. Now the industry has adopted the DVD format, completely reinventing itself again, and appears to be in the process of preparing for another enhanced HDVD format to follow. The film studios have learned that windowing—providing seven or eight different ways of seeing a motion picture—is actually a good thing, and they have benefited enormously from it. "Windowing" means that the very same movie is sent through a release cycle of seven or eight windows of opportunity, from theatrical to premium channels to DVD to video to cable to airplane movies to terrestrial television. Such a format expansion, and the associated update-and-replacement cycle, is the name of the game in the software and video businesses, and something that the music industry needs to pay more attention to, and employ to its full advantage.

So, where are the new audio formats and upgrades? The good old vinyl disc was followed by the 8-track tape, then the cassette tape and the CD. This created a nice cycle of product "upgrades" and industry growth spurts that propelled the industry to greater and greater heights and ever-increasing revenues. The problem is that technology is moving even faster these days, and the music industry has fallen behind. It has been more than twenty years since the CD was first introduced, and the replacement cycle reached its peak in 2000.

Right now, the new audio format is the MP3 file and the best selling disc is a blank, recordable one. Is it possible that the proliferation of MP3 files, an inferior audio format to the CD Red Book standard, might just be giving the music industry new life as more people are exposed to music? Rich Egan, president of indie label Vagrant Records, told *Newsweek* in 2004:

> Five years ago, a record that sold 50,000 copies was a huge success in our world. The standard has totally changed. File-sharing, once thought to be the death knell for the music industry, has actually helped trigger a spending spree. Even MTV and big radio are starting to notice, playing artists they wouldn't have touched three years ago.

Shrinking Retail Space

The decline in the sales of the CD format can also be directly linked to the shrinking amount of square footage available for selling CDs in regional music stores. Over the past five years or so, over twelve hundred traditional CD retailers have closed their doors, driven out of business primarily by a shift in distribution from the traditional record store to mass-market retailers such as Wal-Mart and Best Buy, who significantly discount CDs, often below cost, to drive store traffic. While these low prices have attracted many customers, it has had an impact on other stores around them—and when they close, total square footage available for distribution and diversity of choice goes with them. As a result, many CDs are simply not available for sale at any retail location, sales are missed, and consumers are forced to turn to other means of acquiring music.

Pricing and Value

It is clearly a credible argument that the retail price of a CD is too high to represent a sustained value proposition in the more competitive economic environment. Compare the value of what you get on an $18.95 CD to what you can purchase on a $19.95 DVD, or a $49.99 video game. The DVD, which may have cost millions of dollars to produce and which also contains lots of extra features besides "just" the movie, *appears* to be worth a lot more than a 45- to 70-minute audio recording, and the consumer's perception is simply that you get a lot more value on the DVD. Even with the recent CD-Extra or enhanced CD containing video clips and other supplementary materials, DVDs, and video games just look a lot more hip for the money.

To be fair, the actual street price of many of the most popular CDs has come down considerably, due to the discounted prices by the major retailers, who often sell CDs below cost to attract in-store traffic. However, the record industry seems to have forgotten how to continue to add value to its product as it had done in the past. The music industry may start to take a page or two from their pals in the film and video business. For the past seven or eight years, the movie companies have been busy developing the DVD format, finding new channels to distribute it, all the while slashing its retail price to accelerate the adoption rate and drive market penetration. They have developed an extremely profitable rental business, created compelling video-on-demand offerings, and continued to build even more luxurious movie theaters with surround-sound, vibrating chairs, and plush seating.

During the same time, the music industry has been holding prices steady, and decreasing the breadth of their retail channels, while for a long time refusing to license music to the emerging digital-music players that were pushing the new technologies and business models. The industry lobbied for acts of Congress, including the Record Rental Act of 1985, which outlawed music rentals and the often-decried Digital Millennium Copyright Act of 1998 (DMCA). With this new legislation, the Big Music cartels made it impossible for people to rent records; then, they went straight for the right to invade the privacy of ISPs and their customers. The utter manifestation of the "do what we say or else" paradigm is the RIAA suing people for failing to continue to purchase their overpriced products.

The Changing Face of Music Retail

For years, music stores thrived, selling CDs to an audience eager to both upgrade their existing vinyl music collections and discover some new music. Sales strategies were fairly diverse, and both small and large retailers were able to co-exist. Small shops focused on carrying particular genres of music and catering to the needs of local audiences. Large shops carried a wider mix of genres and provided access to broader constituents. However, even in the best-run music stores, perhaps only ten thousand different titles were available at any given time. That seems like it should be plenty, yet studies have shown that nearly two thirds of all the people who visit a brick-and-mortar record retailer leave the store without finding what they were looking for. Imagine running a clothing store or coffee shop with that rate of customer conversion!

Until about five years ago, the price of a new CD was generally $16.95–$18.95 as a typical street price with occasional discounts on select titles. But things changed when the really large retailers like Costco, Wal-Mart, and Best Buy discovered that they could use music to drive foot traffic into their locations. The major record labels, hungry to expand sales in any way they could, played right into the hands of the monster retailers.

So it's hardly surprising that twelve hundred music retailers have closed their doors in the past few years, and many more are predicted to go out of business. And it's not just the indie record stores. Wherehouse Entertainment, Strawberries, and Tower Records all went bankrupt. "Adapt or die" appears to be the new way for music retailers to survive. Unless a store is in a unique location or designed to derive revenue across a wide variety of products, it is becoming increasingly difficult for music stores to stay in business.

The mass-market retailers, such as Target, Best Buy, Circuit City, and Wal-Mart, truly have changed the landscape of the U.S. retail music channel, accounting for well over 50 percent of all CD sales. By selling a relatively small selection of CDs at heavy discounts, often below their actual wholesale cost, they use them as "loss-leaders" to bring people into the stores to buy other things. These giants have come to gain the largest share of the U.S. market today. Wal-Mart alone accounts for approximately 20 percent of all music sold in the U.S. This is an astonishing figure, given that the music selection at most Wal-Mart stores is usually less than 750 titles deep. Neither the individual music store nor dedicated music chains such as Tower and Virgin can compete with this kind of pricing power.

Despite the massive sales volume that the music industry receives from the mass merchandisers, the sales of these CDs account for less than a couple of percent of overall revenue for these retailers. With Wal-Mart alone, music sales are less than one-tenth of one percent of their revenue. The record companies have become entirely dependent on these giants, but the giants would hardly even miss the sales if they were to decline or disappear entirely. The business strategies of the record labels are no longer aligned with the strategies of their main distribution partners. Could this be a recipe for disaster?

As more stores close, product selection narrows, with only the hits and best sellers actually making it to the shelves. However, this often works hand-in-hand with a label's radio and promotion strategies: focus the efforts on the "sure thing" and take fewer chances. Try getting any attention from your label as a newly signed artist if your first record has not been very successful. Promoting a very narrow range of "proven" artists is more lucrative for the label in the short run, but it leads to increasing homogeneity of the market.

Online sales through the likes of Amazon, Barnes & Noble, and even eBay are also challenging the existence of brick-and-mortar stores. Without the restrictions of shelf space, online stores can offer a much wider selection, making it easy for people to find what they want without ever leaving their home. Sales of CDs have been a consistent source of growth for many online retailers, as they nibble away at traditional music retailers' market shares—and now they are adding digital downloading to the overall shopping experience. Ultimately, retailers will look to sell music any which way that they can, whether it may be fixed media products, or download services to PCs, televisions, or mobile services.

The Future of Music Retailing

Beyond CDs

Even if the best-selling CD prices were reduced to $10 or less, it is questionable whether the current CD format can survive the digital tide, in the long run. It is more likely that another physical format will be created and marketed that just may be compelling enough to compete with digital music stores and providers. Already, almost all of the existing retail music chains have begun to sell DVDs, CD and MP3 players, headphones, books, posters, clothing, merchandise, and other products to supplement constantly declining CD sales.

This is a trend that clearly will continue, with surviving music stores ultimately becoming "lifestyle zones" or "music arcades," where people go to meet a like-minded crowd, and check out all kinds of products that may be associated with their music—and their particular cultural preferences. Music stores positioned to survive in the future are looking a lot more like the retail environment found in Hot Topic stores than the CDs peddlers they were in the past.

As an example, in its twenty-five locations in the greater Boston area, retailer Newbury Comics, long a favorite venue of college kids seeking new music, sells an extremely wide variety of products alongside its CD racks, including comic books, DVDs, posters, toys, and clothing. CEO Mike Dreese says, "We are transforming our stores into temples of cultural junk. We sell to college kids and we carry everything that they are looking for to set up their dorm room . . . everything except the bong."

Many music retailers are already carrying MP3 music players, and it certainly looks like there are going to be many new opportunities for traditional retailers to work with digital distribution companies, such as in-store "filling stations" for digital downloads, custom and fixed-media on-demand manufacturing, accessories, merchandising, and wireless content cards. Napster is already providing a Napster-branded MP3 player to retailers, along with its Toast software and CD burners. Napster also plans to involve retailers to help cross the digital divide, by combining the trust that people have in shopping at brand-name retailers while introducing new customers to digital music. The Virgin Megastore in San Francisco is already offering Mega Play music downloads of any album in the store to your MP3 player, providing sixty or seventy songs for free, as well as frequent buyer programs to customers seeking to sample the latest selections.

Brick-and-mortar music distribution is also no longer exclusively the province of the traditional music store or big-box retailer. Take Starbucks, for instance. The coffee chain started out creating custom compilations of music by big-name artists under its "Hear Music" brand in nearly all of its locations. That effort was so successful that it sparked the evolution of the digital coffeehouse. At ten Starbucks locations in Seattle, and at the Hear Music Coffeehouse in Santa Monica, customers can peruse digital kiosks that provide access to more than 250,000 tracks. They can then burn an album or a personalized mix to CD, all while enjoying their favorite beverage. Starbucks plans to roll out its digital music service to perhaps as many as 2,500 additional outlets over the next few years. Walk into a Starbucks in the near future with your WiFi music player, and say, "Venti latte with a side of light rock."

"Legitimate" Digital Distribution

A number of online digital music distribution services were launched in 2003 and 2004, including iTunes, Rhapsody, Musicmatch, BuyMusic, Wippit, OD2, Sony Connect, Wal-Mart Music Downloads, and the new Napster; and there are many more to come, without a doubt, including MSN and Virgin Digital. At the time of this writing, iTunes offers approximately seven hundred thousand authorized music tracks online (U.S. and U.K. only). Many fewer tracks will be available outside the U.S. and the U.K., due to licensing issues and territorial restrictions that are in effect in most countries. This constitutes less than 8 percent of the active universe of songs (estimated to be eight million), and less than 1 percent of the available music catalog worldwide (estimated at fifty million recordings). This is a pretty good start but still hardly competitive with the virtual mega-libraries of tens of millions of tracks that are offered by the leading P2P exchanges and their "darknet" counterparts, albeit unauthorized.

Compare these numbers with the humble ten thousand CD titles carried in the average record store in the world, and it's easy to understand why the digital distribution of music, whether legal or not, is so appealing to its users. Kazaa's P2P archives, on an average day, offers more than ten million files that are traded online, and this is just one of a growing number of P2P services, despite the lawsuits and the fear-inducing public relations campaigns.

In a true testament to Metcalf's digital network mantra, "the power of a network is exponential to its number of users," these will be very hard numbers for any central-server-based content distribution system to match.

At the same time, the Internet has finally truly reached critical mass, at least in most Western nations. Nearly 60 percent of the American population, 75 percent of the German population, and 82 percent of the Finns are online. Jupiter Research predicts that online music will account for 26 percent of the entire U.S. market, and 5 percent of the market in Europe by the year 2008. Jupiter also forecasts that the U.S. will lead the world's transition to legitimate digital online music services, and that Europe and other areas of the world will lag behind a bit, because of the high P2P usage rates in those territories, and a more difficult legal situation in regards to licensing.

Even then—digital distribution will only account for 50 percent of online activity, according to Jupiter Research. The other 50 percent of the activity will be sales of physical (hard) goods, ordered via the Internet. Furthermore, they are predicting that 75 percent of this activity will be downloads of single, a-la-carte tracks or packaged works (albums), and 25 percent will be subscription-based usage (i.e., flat-fee payments for bulk downloads).

However, in order for any of this to occur, consumers have to get used to *paying* for music services online, and disconnect from the "free" music networks that are so widely available today. If record companies expect people to pay, then they will have to make it much easier and infinitely more convenient and rewarding to buy music rather than to steal it, and must add a lot of other values to be competitive. It is unlikely, either way, that just music "content" in and of itself will bring in sufficient and sustainable revenue streams, so we will likely see the additional cash coming from advertising, sponsorships, merchandising, and indirectly from data-mining and other "Big Brother"–type reporting.

So far, Big Music's own efforts at providing digital music have been experimental, at best, and none of these legitimate services have garnered any real momentum with the customer. Until the release of the Apple iTunes music store, less than a few million tracks had been legitimately downloaded, and even Apple's one hundred million-plus legal downloads at the time of this writing are a mere drop in the bucket compared to the billions of downloads on the P2P networks. After all, how many people are going to spend $10,000 to load up their iPods with ten thousand tracks?

All the same, the iTunes music store has shown strong potential, but it remains to be seen if Apple can indeed ever make money from the "content" itself, rather than using the music to drive the sale of its hardware. Apple has a number of looming challenges, including keeping their iPod price-competitive as other companies bring their online stores and portable music players to market. This is going to be very difficult to do for a company used to high-margin proprietary products.

The other challenge is how to remain relevant. Music is going to be ubiquitous, not tied to a single vendor. Prior to 2004, Apple had steadfastly refused to open up the iPod to be compatible with other online services, preferring instead to control the core technology as it has done with the Macintosh. To their credit, in 2004, they partnered with Hewlett-Packard (HP) and Motorola to embed iTunes technology into HP-branded iPods and Motorola-branded cell phones in a change of strategy that might further advance Apple's music technologies against competitors. The Motorola deal will put iTunes music players in the hands of literally tens of millions of potential Apple customers.

While, on the one hand, Apple appears to be playing nice and making its digital file format compatible with other devices, they are in an all-out format war with Sony, Real Networks, and Microsoft, with all four of these major players pushing their own proprietary file formats. Consequently, there is really no industry-standard digital format among the existing online stores. Microsoft has yet to really hit the gas pedal in this regard, but it remains to be seen which format will ultimately win out.

In July 2004, Real Networks released Harmony, a version of their Rhapsody software that lets customers download files and save them on the iPod. Apple immediately lashed out against Real, claiming that it may have violated the DMCA by hacking the Apple Fair Play file format. Clearly, until digital music companies can come to agreement and create a new universal digital music format that can play across all forms of digital music players, it will be impossible for the overall legitimate downloading market to really take off. Until then, the MP3 format will remain the standard, and free distribution of music may reign supreme.

Having said that, that might not be all that bad for music overall, since selling music is not just a question of distribution. It's a question of service and value, and goes far beyond making certain tracks available on a server. Putting a CD in a rack and waiting for the customer to come and get it is one thing, but putting a track on a Web page and waiting for a customer to come and download it, and pay for that, is quite another. It just does not work the same way. (Content is not turning out to be king, after all. As the parody goes, "Content is king, the customer is King Kong, and service is Godzilla." We think this principle will rule on digital music networks.)

Some of the existing digital music services offer a-la-carte track and album downloading as well as CD burning, while others favor a more hybrid approach, combining streaming, playlist-sharing, downloading, and burning in various subscription bundles. Arguably, in terms of catalog size, none of these paid services effectively compete with what is already available for free from the scorned P2P providers, so a big task looms ahead for the legitimate digital music ventures. The key benefits of paid-for and legal downloading that are being hawked by the current crop of providers—notably including "guaranteed file quality, virus-free songs, and no ads" (yeah, right)—may prove to not be enough to satisfy the majority of customers.

Here's a well-fitting comment from Nobuyuki Idei, über-strategist and Chairman of Sony Corporation, as it appeared in the *Los Angeles Times*, July 2002:

> [The record labels] have to change their mind-set away from selling albums and think about selling singles over the Internet for as cheap as possible—even at 20 cents or 10 cents—and encouraging file-sharing, so they can also get micro-payments for these files. The music industry has to reinvent itself; we can no longer control distribution the way we used to.

Chairman Nobu has hit the nail on the head. Under his model, control is decreased, liquidity is increased, and more money will flow. The key to a healthy new music business is understanding that, unlike the good old days when 100 percent of the revenues were derived from selling "content," selling *just* the music/content in the future is unlikely to contribute more than 50 percent to the bottom line. The rest will be accomplished via advertising, sponsorships, and sales of associated products and services.

What Not to Do: The Criminalization of File-Sharing

The 2003–2004 blizzard of subpoenas filed by the RIAA against individuals involved in file-sharing is a desperate attempt to use a legal hammer to smash the hands of those that "steal" (AKA share) music. The RIAA is especially targeting "super-nodes," heavy users who are the chief file contributors or uploaders on the P2P networks. Whether these lawsuits will prevail seems doubtful, but already, armies of lawyers have been unleashed against the RIAA by their own actions. The issue is also on the radar screen of the U.S. Congress and other legislative bodies around the world. Some of the people who have been targeted by the RIAA are not all that pleased, to put it mildly, and are not necessarily going to go down without a fight.

Jesse Jordan, one of four students initially sued by the RIAA for running file-trading systems at their colleges, settled the case against him for a total of $12,000. On his Web site, he wrote:

> I am to pay the RIAA $12,000. In other words, I am to give them the balance of my bank account—money I have worked over three years to save up. This money was for me to spend on books and other costs that come up from day to day. If the RIAA thinks that this is only a minor setback for me, they are greatly mistaken. I hope that they enjoy the new fax machine (or whatever they plan to spend it on), because the artists they supposedly represent will certainly never see a dime of it . . . It would be a real tragedy to allow the RIAA to stifle the advancement of legitimate peer-to-peer file-sharing services. I will personally make any effort possible to ensure that this repression does not occur . . . If the RIAA thinks that these lawsuits will curb music piracy, they had better think again.

Jordan launched Chewplastic.com (www.chewplastic.com) to solicit comments and to collect donations to defray the settlement costs. At the time of this writing, he had collected all of the $12,000 he was forced to pay to the RIAA.

Jordan settled his case with the RIAA, as have many of the other people sued, but some are fighting the RIAA, and these cases may eventually come to trial. Michele Scimeca, a New Jersey woman also sued by the RIAA, has countersued, claiming that the RIAA violated U.S. anti-racketeering legislation and used extortion and scare tactics to intimidate her into making a settlement. Others may agree with this point of view. In an article that ran in *Insight*, rapper Chuck D of Public Enemy said, "Lawsuits on 12-year-old kids for downloading music, duping a mother into paying a $2,000 settlement for her kid? These tactics are pure Gestapo."

There are privacy and civil liberty issues at risk for the people who have been sued, along with the copyright infringement claims made by the RIAA. There are several ongoing efforts, including those by the American Civil Liberties Union and Verizon, to challenge the RIAA's right to certain information. Many think that the RIAA action is overreaching, and only time will tell as to how things will shake out. But at the time of this writing, the RIAA continues to file suits against anonymous individuals, seeking their identities based on their computer's Internet address.

While many recording artists support the efforts of the RIAA—including Sheryl Crow, Britney Spears, Elton John, Eminem, and Madonna—there are other artists speaking out against the whole idea. "They're protecting an archaic industry. They should turn their attention to new models," says Bob Weir of the Grateful Dead. In *Insight* magazine, David Draiman of the band Disturbed tore into the RIAA following another round of lawsuits. "For the artists, my ass. I didn't ask them to protect me, and I don't want their protection."

New research in 2004 from the Pew Internet Project shows that 60 percent of the musicians/songwriters that they surveyed do not believe that the RIAA's lawsuits will benefit artists or songwriters. When asked what impact free downloading has had on their careers, 37 percent of musicians say that downloading has not really made a difference and 35 percent say it has helped. In addition, 83 percent of the musicians surveyed have provided free samples of their work online and a significant number say free downloading has helped them sell CDs and increase attendance at concerts.

We are beginning to see many instances in which file-sharing is actually helping artists sell out shows and promote new CD releases. "I definitely believe that file-sharing has helped our business," says Guster guitar player Ryan Miller in *USA Today*. "We've sold only a couple hundred thousand copies of each of our last albums. We've never made a cent from our album sales, so we don't really see that money anyway."

According to Alex Ferdinand with Franz Ferdinand in *NME:*

> File-sharing is something that has really helped us as a band in getting established. When we played a gig in New York for the first time, a lot of people there already knew our songs and were singing along. For us it has been global word of mouth that has helped our progress, not hindered it. I don't think it is damaging musicians at all. Downloading music is as revolutionary an invention as the gramophone and I'm all for it.

One thing is certain: the legal actions of the RIAA are not going to defeat those who are seeking a change in the dynamics of the marketplace. Indeed, if anything, the misguided efforts of the RIAA are only encouraging the people who create file-swapping software to accelerate their development efforts. Soon, new software products will make it impossible to track the flow of files from one person to another, or to identity the screen name or IP address of the computer involved. The RIAA cannot win this technological arms race against thousands of programmers that make this their mission.

One such system, Freenet, was born in 2001, the brainchild of Ian Clarke, a student at the University of Edinburgh. Clarke was trying to come up with a secure method for people to swap information online without being traced. His motivation apparently was not to enable the anonymous trading of music files, but instead to make it possible for people in repressed regions like China to evade government agents bent on controlling free speech and the uncensored dissemination of ideas. Clarke's system encrypts the data packets and bounces them through multiple servers so that the origin of the information and its recipients cannot be traced.

File-swapping software vendors are vigorously exploring techniques employed by systems such as Freenet. Michael Weiss, CEO of StreamCast Networks, the parent company of Morpheus, was quoted in the *Boston Globe* as saying, "We are going to provide our users with a measure of security and privacy that will let them feel comfortable on the Internet."

The Digital Kids and the Changing Marketplace

For the past forty-plus years, the prevalent operating mode at record companies throughout the Western world has been to focus on breaking artists that appeal to the youth audience, via radio airplay and record stores. That makes sense, because people under the age of twenty buy 22 percent of all CDs, according to Forrester Research.

The youth market has repeatedly propelled the music business to new heights, from Elvis to the Beatles, from the Monkees to the boy bands, and from Eminem to Britney Spears. Kids make up the single largest group of prospective music consumers, and as a result, music fans over thirty-five had been relegated to the sidelines—a situation that now has changed drastically, with the arrival of file-sharing and digital music services.

At the same time, a radical change has occurred in youth cultures worldwide. This change is beginning to wreak havoc on the traditional assumptions of the industry and on their standard marketing approach. The Internet and digital media technology have become a way of life for most children and teenagers in developed countries, and mass media has become less relevant. This has created a behavioral shift that is one of the primary reasons for the huge popularity of file-sharing.

Along with the still utterly astounding growth of the Internet has come a new, networked mobility exemplified by the explosion of digital music player and cell phone usage, particularly in Europe and Asia. Today's kids are "always-on," natural digeratis, constantly networking, plugged-in and communicating with each other in many unprecedented ways. They are the *screenagers*—and are rapidly changing the way that music is discovered and that business is conducted.

The 'Net Generation

The "'Net Generation," as described by Don Tapscott in his book *Growing Up Digital* (www.growingupdigital.com), is eighty-eight million strong and growing. Comprising the largest group of consumers in North America, these kids are the children of the Baby Boomers. They look at the Internet and fast-speed network connectivity in much the same way that their parents accepted and integrated television and telephones into their lives. Being online and digitally networking with others is the default of many of today's kids.

The 'Net generation, born between 1976 and 1998, represents about 30 percent of the U.S. population, a segment larger than their Baby-Boomer parents. While the Boomers grew up as the TV generation, with Vietnam, Woodstock, the moon landing, and Watergate, the 'Net generation has the Internet, CNN, Iraq, American Idol, a struggling global ecology, and big corporate greed to contend with. They have more information available to them than any group of people on the planet ever had, and they are bathing in content on a daily basis.

These kids have grown up on digital media technologies, and are active and skilled users of video games, cell phones, e-mail, instant messaging, the Web, CDs, and DVDs. Their way of communicating with their friends is profoundly different than that of previous generations. Instant messaging and e-mail have eclipsed many prior means of socializing; for some, online networking has become as popular as actual dating. This generation is far more into interactivity than into passive consumption—couch potatoes have become cyber-networkers.

Kids today distrust mass advertising, and seek out information with much more agility and more proactively than their parents did. Thus, the traditional mass-marketing methods employed by broadcast television and radio have much less impact on this 'Net generation than on their parents. The 'Net generation spends more time online and playing video games than they do watching television. Does this signal the beginning of the end of broadcast television advertising as we know it? Already, the big advertising agencies are doing trials with putting television on the Web. Give this another three to five years, and most companies' advertising budgets will move from television to the Internet.

The Internet and other digital networks have forever changed the equation, in favor of the digitally literate, with the "digital kids" in the lead. Their lives are seamlessly integrated with what they can do online. They form relationships online and create communities where they communicate, learn from one another, interact, participate, play, seek out information from a wide variety of sources, and acquire products and services.

Today's kids take all this technology and its potential for granted, and as they enter the workforce and become more significant spenders, they will have a dramatic impact on how goods and services will be delivered, and on the marketing methods that will prove successful. They spend their time online discovering and searching for stuff they are interested in. The 'Net expands their options in variety, selection, and price. It allows them to sample many products before they purchase and to personalize their selections so that they get what they want. As their spending budgets increase with access to credit and debit cards, Paypal accounts, and online "allowance" systems, there will be no need for Mom or Dad to take them to the mall; they will prefer to transact online.

File-Sharing

As a result, the balance of power is shifting into the hands of the digital kids—the very customers that the records labels are still zeroing in on. The catch is that, in many ways, the prey has become a bit of a hunter, itself. At the beginning of the new millennium, consumer choice rules, and empowered by their digital weapons, the digital kids are increasingly in charge. Now, any music company seeking to reach them and influence their purchasing decisions needs to make sure that their artists' entire online and offline presence is engaging, entertaining, rewarding, and highly interactive.

Arguably, file-sharing is the most successful and direct form of product sampling ever invented. It grew out of actual online behavior, and was incubated and created by the digital kids themselves. Shawn Fanning, the brain and inventor of the original Napster, was simply trying to improve the way that he saw file trading being undertaken via Internet Relay Chats. (Fanning was eighteen at the time and a huge music fan.) File-sharing has exploded in popularity since then, because it has become very easy to do and it supports self-directed and collaborative musical exploration. Of course, this is just the tip of the iceberg. Many digital kids know how to write HTML code, create software, and harness the power of the Internet—and they will be adapting it to their benefit.

File-sharing has become the most popular way for people to find out about music, with over 75 percent of the teenagers in the U.S.

engaging in it. This is a definitive glimpse of the future of music and media marketing. A 2003 Harris Interactive survey of teens showed that roughly three out of four teens feel that it should be legal to share music files with each other without making any extra payments to the rights holders. It's just as well that they feel that way, because many kids do not have access to credit cards. Former Napster president Mike Bebel claims that the lack of access to credit cards has been a "significant barrier to the legitimate digital music market." The feels-like-free music offered via the many P2P systems is just too good to pass up. For kids, downloading free music looks like harmless fun—and there has yet to be a definitive study that confirms the record industry's claims that CD sales are negatively impacted by free downloading.

Kids are as passionate about music today as they have ever been, or maybe even more so. More music has been sampled, edited, copied, and shared in the past two or three years than ever before. A 2004 poll of children ages eight to eighteen by Harris Interactive showed that 56 percent of American teenagers with Internet access said that they download music on a regular basis, even though they know that they are breaking the law. Is this just because the music is free, or because these kids are really interested in music? After all, a lot of things are free and still don't have the draw that music does.

Big Champagne, a provider of statistical information on download communities and file-sharing networks, estimates that more files are being downloaded *each month* across the various networks than are being sold by the music industry on an *annual basis*, a factor of 12 to 1. This ratio is expanding, and by the time you read this book, it will most likely be significantly higher.

File-sharing has become the most popular way for kids to get their music, and the file-sharing community is the largest marketplace on the planet. It is the international listening station of choice. Figures from the Pew Internet and American Life Project show that the number of regular music downloaders is growing at a rate of over 100 percent annually. How can and will this potential be put to good use? When will music companies realize that this virtual community is the biggest marketing opportunity they have ever seen—not the largest community of criminals?

If you talk to today's teenagers about music, their feelings and attitudes are quite different than that of the thirty/forty-somethings, who (like the writers of this book) were brought up before the digital era and before any of this was even on the horizon. The kids' culture is a highly mobile, networked, all-digital, and interactive culture, and digital technologies are a tacit standard that is completely and unobtrusively integrated into their lifestyles. Radio used to be where the kids heard new songs, but today they largely feel that radio has become a monotonous top-40 loop, and that it has mutated into a giant advertising delivery machine. Many stations play the same songs over and over—no wonder, since many of them are centrally programmed.

So, the kids turn to the 'Net, which they use for many hours every day as a "next-generation radio," digging for new music and finding their own treasures. Here, they feel that they can control and select what they are going to hear, rather than waiting for a show to start on television or listening to the canned radio programming. They don't just download or stream hundreds of songs; they also visit artist sites, send text messages, find out about shows, listen to online radio, get most of their information on their favorite bands, trade files with their friends via instant messaging and SMS, and have created their own ways to find out about new music. This is a completely new way of discovering music and hanging out with your peers in a free-form, digital environment. What kid wouldn't like that?

To them, file-sharing is a great way to test a song or an artist. Many kids eventually buy the CDs, and many do not—just like it was in the days of trading vinyl and recording the music on cassette tapes.

Too Much Money

Many kids think that $10 or less would be a fair price to pay for a new release on CD (and less for back-catalog items!), and they are increasingly unlikely to buy a lot of music at higher prices. Many of them, perhaps millions, willfully pay $2–$5 for a burned disc from a friend in their high school cafeteria or college dorm. A full 70 percent of kids surveyed say there would be a lot less downloading of music if the price of CDs were lower, according to Harris Interactive. Would a change in pricing wipe out file-sharing? Is this downward pricing pressure created by the 'Net the same as we have already witnessed in airline travel and hotels?

Kids have mixed views about "taking" an artist's music without making a payment. "They're not losing money, because we still buy the t-shirts and go to their concerts. They're still famous," said a 14-year-old girl in a *New York Times* article (March 2004). But for the most part, today's kids already know that most of the artists they like are ultimately not the "real" beneficiaries of their CD purchases, anyway—the record companies and their corporate owners are, and that leaves a sour taste in kids' mouths.

The younger the kids, the more likely they are to not care about "copyright" issues. In fact, they have no real idea what copyright means to begin with, which is not surprising, given the maze of legal obscurities and public propaganda that surround copyright, courtesy of Big Music and Big Mouse. However, many kids do have a hunch that some sort of copyright scheme is a good thing and necessary for the creator of the music, and most would readily agree that *the artists* should get paid. But they also think the industry fat cats—the middlemen—are just too rich, too stuck up, and too self-important to care. Who can blame kids for having this attitude? To them the record industry really does seem to deserve it, they reason, given the public image the industry has created for itself.

Mixed Messages: Have Your Cake and Eat It, Too?

While downloading digital music and other content is now a huge part of the sales pitch for personal computers and other hardware from Apple, Dell, Gateway, and others, the music industry is busy suing people who do so, fair-use rights be damned. Back in 2000, Apple set off an uproar within the music industry with its "Rip, Mix, Burn" ad campaign. Today, iTunes is the most popular music service in the world. Kids wonder, "Which way is it: can I use these cool tools and machines to do what I want, or not? Why do they sell PCs with CD burners, WiFi hubs, and DSL deals if it's really illegal to download stuff from the 'Net, copy CDs, or to share files?" Even Sony—a company that sells music—also offers computers and consumer electronics devices that can play, download, copy, and store music, including audio players that can play CDR discs filled with hours of anything-goes MP3 files. Looking more closely, however, Sony makes only 8 percent of its global turnover by selling music, so it is hardly surprising that the hardware people steer the ship. The message from the entertainment and consumer electronics industries is indeed hot and cold: Use our devices to express yourself, but don't change the rules of the content industries.

Oldies but Goldies

And of course, the youth market is not the only strong market for the future of music. In fact, it is likely to diminish in importance over the next twenty-five years. Already, there are hundreds of millions of adults online, networking just like the digital kids, and while our habits and reliance on the Internet and the style of networking varies from the kids, we are nonetheless online, armed with credit cards, Paypal accounts, and dozens of passwords and cookies.

Recent National Association of Record Merchants (NARM) data shows that female consumers accounted for 53 percent of CD sales, outnumbering men. NARM also reported recent growth in sales to the older demographics, while the 13- to 17-year-old category lost relative market share. Apple reported that every track in their iTunes catalog had been purchased at least once, indicating the good possibility of a broadening of the target age demographic for music buyers. Although Big Champagne says the most popular downloads are usually the ones being pushed by the record labels, they also say there is a broad and diverse mix of files being traded—ubiquity may beget diversity, after all?

Music Companies Must Embrace the Digital Future

How can a 14-year-old who has an allowance of $5 a week feel bad about downloading music produced by multimillionaire-musicians and greedy record companies? The record companies should approach that 14-year-old and say: "Hey it's great that you love music. Instead of downloading music for free, why don't you try this very inexpensive service that will enable

you to listen to a lot of music and also have access to unre-
leased tracks and ticket discounts and free merchandise?"

—Moby, musician, on his Web site

Today, the more artists can reach out to their fans—especially, the kids—via the 'Net, the better off everyone will be. To resist the rise of file-sharing is to ignore the fact that finally, there is a way to reach a huge audience nearly for free with whatever music you have to offer. As the saying goes, the rising tide will float all boats. Those who try and stop it will be washed overboard in the floodwaters, never to be seen again. Those who learn to ride the rising waters and navigate the flowing current will be carried onto a better world where artists and fans of music can connect more fluidly.

Many new file-sharing systems have been developed since the original Napster. The digital kids themselves wrote most of this software—witness Shawn Fanning. These systems are now evolving to include community features such as chat, people- and taste-matching, more sophisticated search tools, and ways for users to browse the collections and playlists of other people who have similar tastes in music.

Today the power of digital referrals and word-of-*mouse* marketing via file-sharing has eclipsed traditional radio marketing on a global scale. Instant messaging, chat, and e-mail have created amazing communication opportunities—pen pals on steroids. These social environments allow anytime/anywhere access to like-minded people to collaborate, share knowledge, and everything else, including music. We must get used to the idea of this free flow of information being the norm rather than the exception. We must realize how the power of online networking contributes to the fulfillment of the needs and desires of the digital kids, especially once it intertwines with offline, "real-life" events and experiences. Kids seeking autonomy and a sense of self can find some of that online, as weird as that may sound to some of us. The 'Net can satisfy their curiosity and their desire to seek identity through online peer groups, which help create a sense of belonging and purpose. To a large extent, this is what's happening with instant messaging.

In the future, the opportunity to influence, and thus market to, large groups will lie squarely with the ability to reach them quickly, inexpensively, and of course *virally,* via peer groups and via the smart leveraging of social networks. Radio play, advertising, street teams, events, and many other traditional forms of marketing are going to fit right next to new forms of peer-to-peer digital marketing. Creating a buzz has always been essential in the promotion of music. Exposure begets discovery, which begets income. Smart marketers will try to compete with free music and enable the kids to transact easily, much as Apple is doing with its iTunes "allowance" and as Napster 2 is doing with its prepaid download cards distributed at major retailers. Smart Web sites, cell phones, and network savvy applications are where it is at in the future of music marketing to the digital kids.

A New Music Economy

Long Time Gone: A Perfectly Broken System

The music business has been based on a star model since its inception. The RIAA confirms that less than 10 percent of recording artists ever recoup their royalty advances, and even that number is wishful thinking, really. Of the approximately thirty-two thousand new CDs released each year, only 250 sell more than ten thousand copies, and fewer than thirty go platinum (one million units sold, in the U.S.). That's 1/10 of 1 percent of the new releases (0.001). Sort of like playing the lottery, except if you're the artist, you're betting with your life—and the odds may indeed be better with the lottery.

Only 15 percent of the musicians who are members of the American Federation of Musicians union have steady gigs in music, and the 273,000 working musicians in America make an average of $30,000 a year—compare that to a cab driver's income. Of course, the real steady money in the music business is in publishing, where songwriters, due to the compulsory mechanical royalty on all records sold and the revenues that flow from public performance, can often make a decent living over a reasonable period of time—nickels and dimes from a multitude of sources.

Most record companies today market artists based on a "see if it sticks" approach. They put a hundred different artists on the market, knowing that less than five of them will ever break even. They hope for that one act that will hit the big-time so that they recoup the entire investment across their whole roster of acts—not much different than a venture capitalist who invests in thirty companies with the hope that one of them will grow to be the next Netscape. Looking back, one could convincingly argue that artist development declined long before the Internet assault on the music business began. The CD replacement cycle that saw many of the fans buying the same music on CD, again, caused an unexpected ten-year boom for the record companies, and this boom was largely based on reissuing existing catalog in the high-quality CD format.

Artist development and the idea of nurturing a career gave way to a herd mentality, in which label executives scrambled to chase and repeat the success of someone else's combination of talent, timing, and good luck. Remember the disco explosion that followed Donna

Summer's early hits, or the rush to sign Grunge bands from Seattle after Nirvana broke big, or the boy bands of the 1990s, or the *American Idol* and revived *Star Search* television shows of today.

In addition, the consolidation and concentration of record labels into the hands of a few large conglomerates, and the deterioration of radio playlist diversity brought on by that industry's deregulation, has made the industry even more risk-averse than ever. With the exception of EMI, and more recently Warner, the major music labels are but small subsidiaries of huge corporations, and it often seems that the actual *music* no longer really matters in their day-to-day decision making. According to Joni Mitchell, in a *Rolling Stone* interview, "I hope it all goes down the crapper. I would never take another deal in the record business . . . I'll be damned if I'll line their pockets."

Still, the Internet and other digital content networks have taken the lid off the record business. The veil of secrecy and nepotism has been removed, exposing the uniquely bizarre behavior that is still prevalent in this business, plain for all to see. Once pioneering artists such as Todd Rundgren, Prince, Aimee Mann, and Peter Gabriel realized that they no longer needed to be the chips in the record industry's poker game, things began to change. Digital content networks now provide the opportunity and exposure for artists to drive their own careers, as musicians and artists, without being under the de-facto control of an international cartel.

During the first decade of online music, the incumbent music companies were not sure how to handle the many issues associated with selling music online, and most major players simply held out, and stayed put, in order to eke out the best possible deal. Most notable were the major labels that, for a long time, basically refused to license their catalogs to the early entrants into the digital space. A lot of song and dance went on, but few deals were closed, and even fewer actually allowed for any real business to happen. The result: music fans flocked to unlicensed services.

The labels wanted to keep the control of *all* pieces of this puzzle, at all times, simply because they felt that it was, after all, "their" recordings that were being downloaded and used as the prime force in this business. Then again, this view has now been proven wrong: content *in and of itself* is *not* king, and is no longer the sole reason that people will give the music guys their hard-earned cash. As we said earlier, content is king, the customer is King Kong, and service is Godzilla—that could well be the mantra of the days to come. The next few pages will describe some of the bright spots in the future of music and will help us think about new ways of reconfiguring the music business and the artist/fan relationship.

Pennies from Heaven

Publishing and all kinds of licensing will likely be digital cash-cows for artists and writers, in the future even more so than today. New contract constructs and agency-type deals are likely to approach the digital transaction from a licensing point of view rather than from a "work for hire" standpoint. Artists may stop doing business with record labels that have become outmoded dinosaurs. Ultimately, within the next five to eight years, the legitimate music downloading services such as iTunes and Rhapsody have enormous potential to generate substantial revenue, and very likely, the pie will only be larger, with more pieces for everyone. But the real question is: *who will get the money?* When credit card and payment companies make a larger share than the artist, something clearly is wrong.

The prevailing business model of publishing, in which royalties are collected and administered on behalf of the songwriter, still has a firm place in the future, as long as people will spend money (or its equivalent) for music—and it's safe to assume that they will, under the right circumstances. Although the actual methods of distribution may vary, it remains the mission and duty of the publisher to ensure that a writer's work is heard and seen, and that they are paid for it, one way or another. While mechanical reproduction income from CD sales will likely drop further, there is significant potential for this revenue stream to be bolstered with the legitimate download model.

The digital network itself will benefit writers and artists because sales and/or uses are much easier to accurately track and report. Currently, most performing rights organizations still rely on human estimates, averaging, and sampling. For example, the royalties paid on music played in restaurants is based on the same sample data as radio airplay, and surely that data is skewed because no consideration is given for the more likely ethnic diversity of music played in restaurants. Digital technologies could enable this to be much more accurate.

Independent Labels

Independent and smaller artist-owned labels are usually structured so that they can survive with much lower sales and turn a profit by employing niche-marketing methods. Thus they are less threatened than the large record labels. In the past, the independent labels were agreeable to licensing their catalogs to legitimate music download services when major labels stalled. Smaller labels are also better able to focus on developing the careers of their artists. Their smaller size also will help them to remain flexible, as they will be able to adapt and re-tool their business models when necessary. More than ten thousand independent labels exist today, with many more on the way. This is extremely good news for the music business.

Most of the innovation in music has always come from the independent labels that were willing to take risks. When rock 'n' roll exploded on the scene in the mid-1950s, major labels scorned it. However, basement concerns like Chess and Sun made fortunes. Likewise, no one initially saw a buck in disco except Casablanca Records; again, millions were made. More recently, rap, hip-hop, country, and to a lesser extent, reggae, illustrate the same story. Major record labels are often too large and ponderous to be in a position to discover and nurture great musicians during the early phases of their careers. Independents worldwide have been and will continue to be the lifeblood of the music industry, and most significant musical trends have had their origins in small independent music labels.

The Billboard charts of the last few years show an interesting and somewhat surprising trend. Thanks to the installation of point-of-sale systems at major music chain retailers, SoundScan's computers can poll music stores and get the exact number of each title sold. Prior to SoundScan, sales were tracked by a questionable method of manually polling music chains, wholesalers, and independent record stores—a process that highly favored the major record labels.

By 1991, three indie labels had entered the list of top-twenty labels, placing nineteen titles on the Billboard 200 for 5.1 percent of the label chart share. By 1992, the indie labels represented thirty-four titles on the chart. The trend is even more dramatic if we look at Billboard's Top R&B Albums chart, where the indies' share doubled between 1990 and 1992, to a total of 22.2 percent. During one week in 1996, indie-label bands occupied all top five spots on the chart!

Majors today seem to act more like film distributors than production houses. They have the organization, the capital, and the clout to take new music to the broad public, but little ability to develop the next hot artists, themselves. Indies are the highly valued testing grounds for the superstars of tomorrow.

"While the majors want to sell music like McDonald's sells hamburgers, we'd rather be a small chain of gourmet restaurants with a line going around the block," says Bruce Iglauer, founder of indie label Alligator Records. "It's the menu that counts—not how many are served." Independent labels are artistically and creatively on the cutting-edge of the new music, and new music is not a fad; it is the fastest-growing segment of the music market. It includes everything from rap, urban, and alternative to country, world, and folk.

Growing market segmentation by musical style is another significant factor for independent labels. Rock's share of music sales, so long the mainstay of pop music, has plunged 27 percent since 1987 to about 32 percent of the total. This new musical diversity is reflected in the Grammy awards, which started in 1959 with a mere twenty-eight categories. That number has grown to nearly one hundred.

A rapidly segmenting music market means more opportunity for independents whose releases detail the richness of particular niche musical forms: the blues of Black Top and Alligator, the rap of Priority and Ruffhouse, the industrial dance meshes of Nettwerk and Wax Trax, the world folk of Green Linnet, the rock 'n' roll of Touch 'n' Go—the list goes on and on.

Many of these companies didn't just find a niche and fill it, as so many lesser New Age and "fuzak" labels do, nor did they just concoct one and market it, like so many major-label-forged "alternative" indies. They usually developed their label along with the music they presented, often as a hobby, bringing bands and artists to an ardent audience and then riding the crest of their influence. For a number of the smarter and luckier indies, yesterday's hobby has become today's gold mine.

Record retail is only part of the story. Independents have long known that the most effective way to reach their niche audiences is to go direct via mail and now, of course, via the Internet. Direct marketing of music recordings accounts for about 10 percent of overall sales in the U.S. for major labels, but up to 50 percent of sales for independents! Other record retail alternatives include bookstores, record clubs, specialty gift stores, and television home shopping.

Going forward, music will increasingly be direct marketed and distributed on digital networks. It is now possible to reach an audience directly and use the Internet to deliver the music, or leverage the almost daily-appearing digital music distribution services that are exploding online. Here, it is more important than ever to develop a loyal fan base and meaningful customer relationships. "The accelerating trend," says Davitt Sigerson, former president of Island Records, "is putting much more control in the hands of the public, and much less control in the hands of the tastemakers and gatekeepers."

Sanctuary Group

Sanctuary Group, PLC is terrific example of a well-run musician business providing a network of connected companies that address all aspects and opportunities in the music industry. It is perhaps the model for the music company of the future, with 360-degree participation of all the related revenue streams meaningful to artists. Sanctuary businesses include recorded music, visual entertainment, artist and producer management, tour support, live booking, music publishing and licensing, new media, marketing services, recording studios, book and DVD publishing, and merchandising.

Sanctuary has achieved impressive growth by focusing on established artists with a substantial fan base and providing them with all the services and support they could possibly need. While most of the major record labels were dumping acts by the dozens, with some artists running screaming from them, Sanctuary has been steadily picking up the established acts with staying power and loyal fans. Sanctuary has focused mightily on developing their artist services businesses—management, live booking, and merchandising—across a wide spectrum of artists. This strategy is paying off and positions them as a potential long-term survivor. They are filling the vacuum left by the major labels with a more enlightened business model, based on a philosophy of artist management.

Sanctuary is the U.K.'s largest independent record company focused on producing music and DVDs for their artists. Their catalog includes Morrissey, the Libertines, Kiss, Lynyrd Skynyrd, Spiritualized, the Strokes, Widespread Panic, Ween, Blondie, Neil Young, Crosby-

Nash, Alison Moyet, the Delays, Small Faces, and Fun Lovin' Criminals, across over twenty labels. DVD titles include the Who, Iron Maiden, and Rush. But far more than just a record label, Sanctuary provides a host of services to artists seeking success in the music business.

Their artist management teams represent Beyoncé, Destiny's Child, Mary J Blige, Judas Priest, the Who, Groove Armada, Guns N' Roses, Iron Maiden, Fleetwood Mac, the Von Bondies, Jane's Addiction, Slayer, Slipknot, and others. They also manage music producers, including John Alagia, Bob Ezrin, Ethan Johns, and Chris Neil. Sanctuary now owns the largest live booking agency outside the U.S., booking some seven thousand shows last year and reporting a very healthy marketplace for live music. The booking agency handles tours for lots of bands, including Robbie Williams, the Darkness, Dido, Eminem, Red Hot Chili Peppers, Metallica, Coldplay, Marilyn Manson, and 50 Cent. Sanctuary also runs an in-house travel agency and tour production company, which provide tour logistics for their managed acts.

The Bravado company sells merchandise on live tours, at retail outlets, and on the Web. Bravado claims to be the fastest growing entertainment merchandiser in the world today, representing Christina Aguilera, Robbie Williams, Eminem, 50 Cent, Iron Maiden, Led Zeppelin, N.E.R.D., Elton John, Hilary Duff, Beyoncé, Jane's Addiction, and Oasis. Bravado can provide artists with lots of opportunities to sell things, including ring tones, branded games and wallpapers for mobile phones, as well as the usual T-shirts and posters.

Founded in 1979 as a management company for Iron Maiden, the Sanctuary Group has been on a financial tear for the past years, expanding revenues from £23 million in 1999 to £152 million in 2003, all the while being very profitable. And we thought the music business was in trouble?

www.sanctuarygroup.com

Live Performance and Touring

While CD sales were falling over the last four to five years, the popularity of live shows, festivals, and concerts has been increasing every year, and revenues from big-ticket concerts have grown steadily. For musicians in the pop and rock genres, the chance of making a living in the traditional CD-sales based "record business" is rapidly dwindling—but maybe that's a good thing. After all, that elusive major-label record deal all too often proved to be a pyrrhic victory, anyhow, since only 4 percent of records ever sold enough copies to break even.

Perpetual obscurity would thus seem to be the default destiny for many of today's musicians, if it were not for the "music like water" paradigm changes described in this book. This new paradigm—in which music changes from product to service, and musicians derive greater exposure and income from live performance, digital performances, and other revenue streams than they do from CD sales—will not be as daunting for jazz and classical musicians, for example, who are accustomed to earning most of their money from live performance anyway.

Is this where the music industry is heading, in a digital future? Back to earning a living "with your feet" and hitting the road to make a buck, in order to find and reach your audience? Yes and no. We think that many aspects of digital music (and "digital music marketing") and live entertainment will be converging down the road, and that the two sectors will be much more intertwined than music/CD retail and touring could ever have been. Why? Because *digital music is mobile*, and as intangible and experience-based as the concert experience. In fact, because of digital technologies, we may well see the manager and agents of the future take on some distribution and product marketing tasks, as well, and thus further decimate the importance of the traditional record company.

Historically, the music retail business seems to have developed on a separate tangent from the live music industry, with a different view on how money is made and shared, a different breed of people working in it, and with its own conventions, events, and trade shows. As a result, we have two rather different segments within one industry, but this will rapidly be amalgamated in the digital environment. Digital music companies will have to take a much more inclusive view of the music industry landscape, and will quickly seek to harvest a lot of synergistic revenues. Live music promoters and agents have always been much closer to the artists and to their audiences (i.e., the ticket-buyers and concert-goers), so it is only natural that they would recognize the shifts in the marketplace and act accordingly.

Technology has long been embraced wholeheartedly in the concert and touring business, whether it is in the production sectors (lights, sound, multimedia), logistics (booking and accounting, communications), or the marketing of the shows (e-mail, online tickets, market research, etc.), and many cutting-edge applications of technology have emerged. New services like Boston's SonicBids (www.sonicbids.com) allow concert promoters to gauge their target audience in various markets, and thus avoid booking shows in locations that are less likely to work with any specific act.

Most importantly, since the concert business has always been an experience business, its executives and managers have always been required to stay very much in touch with their customers to avoid costly disconnects and productions that did not succeed in getting the attention of the marketplace. Customer empowerment is already a default setting in the concert business: the customer calls the shots, and always gets what he wants. We saw this clearly in the summer of 2004 in the U.S., where customers actually turned away from popular shows because of the sky-high ticket prices promoters had set. This has caused the concert business to reassess the advances and guarantees paid to artists and realign their pricing strategy to the clear signal from the buying public. Compare that to the traditional record business, which is essentially internally oriented. In the record business, a few companies and their moguls have dictated the terms that the "user" must adhere to, or else forget about the music.

Sadly, but not surprisingly, customer empowerment is not what the record business has been all about, and if the record business can take a few pages from the concert business, it would be much better off. But it may be a case of "too little, too late." The record business of tomorrow may have left itself wide open to a takeover by the agents and managers. Imagine the strategy-room whiteboards in those big music agencies!

The record industry, in its obsession with mass marketing, huge profit margins, and top-down domination, has gradually but steadily grown detached from its artists and, even worse, from its fans and consumers. There is very little direct communication between the people who run record companies and the people who buy their records, and it shows. The disconnect runs so deep that record companies actually thought they could get away with suing their own customers without consequence for looking elsewhere to get their needs met. The real "music guys" in the record business have come and gone—with notable exceptions such as Clive Davis and Quincy

Jones—and the ships are now captained by corporate functionaries who could just as well be running Novartis, Toys "R" Us, or Starbucks.

While the record industry has grown isolated and out-of-touch in its New York high-rises, Hollywood Jacuzzis, or the golf courses surrounding Guetersloh, Germany (home of Bertelsmann, of BMG), the concert industry has had to face the tough reality of what people will *actually* buy, and for how much, day in and day out. While many joke that music publishers practically "make money in their sleep," collecting royalties from the performance and use of their songs in far-away places without having to actually be there themselves, the concert business works every single show, right there, in person, in real time.

The concert promoters and venue owners like Clear Channel are already distributing live recordings of the shows directly to the audience as they leave the venue. Artists including Phish, the Allman Brothers Band, Peter Gabriel, the Who, String Cheese Incident, Primus, Dave Matthews, Duran Duran, Moe, and Incubus have all experimented with delivering live shows via the Internet, and many are finding it quite lucrative. You can get the show on CD, directly download it to a portable USB key drive, or download it off the venue or band Web site when you get home. In the near future, you will be able to collect a real-time stream of a live performance you are listening to directly to your WiFi-enabled device, and take it home with you.

This live interaction and integrated music experience, combined with the Web and the power of direct marketing and community building, is about to blow the doors off all previous forms of music marketing and distribution. The record companies are getting broadsided by their buddies in the concert business, who appear to be set on increasing revenues at the expense of those asleep at the wheel.

Merchandising

Artist merchandising stands to benefit nicely from the digital transformation of the music business. Direct marketing is the Web's way of selling, and it's certainly easier than having fans wait in line at a show—it also helps to form a richer and more direct consumer relationship. For many years, music merchandising was simply the business of selling hats and t-shirts to fans at concert venues. These days, the very nature of music merchandising is undergoing a very positive transformation, and it is now more about the marriage of music, culture, creative marketing, and fashion. Jimmy Buffet built an empire of restaurants on the "Margueritaville" theme, and got into tequila distribution and frozen foods alongside his sold-out concerts and CDs. Applying entrepreneurial thinking to the development of "musician businesses" often includes a redefinition of merchandising—and it is creating a new industry that transcends the notion that the only way to make money in music is to record and perform. One only has to look at the success of Def Jam and Bad Boy Entertainment to see the power that music marketing and merchandising have in driving all kinds of new forms of revenue for artists.

The Hip-Hop Phenomenon and the Rise of the New Moguls

Hip-hop culture has become a de-facto part of mainstream culture through the combined power of music, merchandise, and marketing. Brands such as Baby Phat, Roc-A-Wear, Sean Jean, Phat Farm, Shady, and Snoop Dogg are among the leading brands of hip-hop-inspired clothing and merchandising businesses, and are making many of hip-hop's smartest artists very wealthy. According to Simmons Lathan Media Group, 45.3 million consumers worldwide spend $12.6 billion annually on hip-hop media and merchandise. The hip-hop success formula has a lot more to do with creating far-reaching musician businesses than just selling CDs.

Entrepreneur Russell Simmons spearheaded hip-hop culture's move to the mainstream with Def Jam Records in the '80s, and has since expanded into marketing, fashion, theater, and jewelry. Sean "Puffy" Combs began developing recording artists as a teen. Within two decades, he had parlayed his skills into a multifaceted, multimillion-dollar empire that includes his own record label, clothing line, and restaurant chain. Jay-Z has clothing company Roc-A-Wear, a Vodka distribution business, and another joint venture with Reebok to market his S. Carter Collection sneakers. Hip-hop artists Simmons, L.L. Cool J, Missy Elliott, Eminem, Ludacris, Nelly, Sean Combs, and Jay-Z have shown corporate America that hip-hop can generate substantial dollars outside the recorded music industry. They have parlayed their early success in the record business into powerful empires that they control.

Hot Topic

Founded in 1989, Hot Topic, Inc. seized the potential of fusing music videos, alternative artists, and teenage fashions. Over the past fifteen years, the company has built a powerful merchandising empire around this concept. At Hot Topic stores, you can find a huge assortment of street wear, retro-influenced lounge, punk, club, and Gothic clothing and merchandise, including lingerie, hosiery, cosmetics, belts, handbags, shoes, body jewelry, make-up, rings, shoes, gifts, furniture, candles, magazines, vinyl and CDs, action figures, and more.

Hot Topic features clothing and merchandise for a wide array of bands: AC/DC, Black Sabbath, Deftones, Disturbed, Godsmack, Green Day, Incubus, Insane Clown Posse, Iron Maiden, Judas Priest, Kid Rock, Korn, Linkin Park, Machine Head, Marilyn Manson, Megadeth, Metallica, Mötley Crüe, Motorhead, Ozzy, Pantera, Papa Roach, Rage Against the Machine, Slayer, Slipknot, Staind, Stone Temple Pilots, System of a Down, Taproot, and many others. While they don't sell much in the way of actual music at the moment, they have taken merchandising to a new level of sophistication.

Proving the power of using music to sell merchandise, the company had 2004 revenues of $572 million and earnings of $48 million. It operates more than 550 mall-based stores throughout the United States and Puerto Rico, as well as the Hot Topic and Torrid Web sites (www.hottopic.com and www.torrid.com). Hot Topic is well positioned to become a retail platform that takes advantage of the evolution of the music business.

Mixtapes, MP3 Blogs, and File-Sharing

While major label representatives officially decry the evil of file-sharing, one can see that the inherent behavior involved has been going on for some time, often with the endorsement of the major labels themselves, even if unofficially. Music compilations originally on cassette and now on CDs are widely used in the hip-hop and other music communities to help create a "buzz . . . before a single goes to radio," says Courtney Powell, Elektra's director of rap promotions and street marketing. To achieve that buzz, Powell will pass a song along to one hundred mixtape DJs, according to a 2003 article in the *Boston*

Globe. The proliferation of this free music has propelled the careers of many artists including 50 Cent, Eminem, Beyoncé, and Ludacris.

The label people in the promotion and marketing departments actually enable and encourage this infringement of copyright in order to grease the skids and help break the songs. The DJs that make the mixtapes and help lubricate the wheels of commerce are integral to the marketing and credibility of a new song or artist in the hip-hop community. Mixtapes made by DJs including Kay Slay, Envy, Green Lantern, Whoo Kid, Clue, and other "streets" set the pace for what is hip and what is not. MTV even features the medium in their "Mixtape Mondays" segments. You can buy the bootleg CDs from friends, DJs, local retailers, or online at mixtapesusa.com, buymixtapes.com, and mixtapeskings.com. Illegal, yes, but powerful and important to breaking a song in the hip-hop genre.

While the RIAA rattles its swords at illegitimate file-sharing and free music in general, the labels nevertheless find both to be extremely effective promotional vehicles. On one side, it is clearly a demonstration of the power of free music as a promotion; the fact that the labels themselves feed the mixtape machine is indicative of its effectiveness. There are also many anecdotes of tracks "leaked" to the Internet by people inside the record companies, days or weeks before the street date of the CD. Warner Records actually asked several MP3 blogs to post tracks from rock band Secret Machines in August 2004.

On the other hand, the music industry relies on a shaky defense that puts the copying and distribution responsibility on the shoulders of the DJs that produce the mixtapes. There have been raids on small stores that sell mixtapes, and some DJs have been arrested. However, soon after, the beat goes on and the genre is once again alive with the proliferation of illegally leaked, duplicated, and distributed mixtapes that fuel the buzz and subsequent acceptance of new tracks into the marketplace.

Long before the Internet, people used to pass tapes of bands that I've never gotten to see live and fall in love with them. And I think the Internet is an easy way to do that, to really turn people on.

—Jason Mraz, musician, in *Teen Music*

CD Pricing

For a long time, people have been complaining about the high price of CDs, and they have voted with their feet by choosing to purchase music at the huge discounts offered by mass merchants such as Best Buy. These big-box retailers made it very difficult for stand-alone CD stores to compete. In an effort to prop up the independent music stores, Universal, the largest of the major record labels, announced price cuts in the summer of 2003. The cuts, which took effect in October 2003, slashed CD pricing from $17–$19 list to $12.95. While this is a long overdue move on the part of the major labels, most people believe that it is too little, too late. Jim Urie, president of Universal music and video distribution, said at the time, "Music sales needed a jump-start. We needed to get people back in stores and into the habit of paying for music." This statement fits neatly with the party line that, basically, online file-sharing is responsible for killing the industry. Jim appears to forget the proven fact that people have always liked that $10–$12 price point, and have been paying that much for music at the mass merchandisers for some time.

This price cut has been carried out in typical major-label fashion. Along with the introduction of the new pricing model, Universal also slashed the co-op marketing money and positioning fees they had paid to the retailers to promote their records. Universal claims that they will instead direct the money toward their own radio, television, and print advertising campaigns. However, many retailers around the country relied on these marketing funds to promote their stores, with many of them netting more money from these fees than they did from selling CDs. While consumers could be the biggest beneficiaries of the price cuts in the short run, the retailers could end up being the biggest losers. And if brick-and-mortar retail channels continue to shrink, there will be even fewer places for people to purchase CDs, leading to even fewer choices on the shelves and an even greater migration to the digital networks.

The voices of the industry clearly tell the story. Anne Garbus, owner of a chain of music stores in Michigan that will close because of declining sales, told the *Chicago Tribune*:

We've been telling the major labels for years that they're priced too high, and we were told to stop whining. I applaud them for finally listening to consumers. But it's too late for the 600 record stores that closed last year, it's too late for places like Tower Records, and it's too late for me.

In the same paper, Mike Dreese, CEO of Newbury Comics, said:

As technologies emerge that allow consumers to run their lives better, faster, smarter, there is no doubt that the utter digitization of it all will lead to a place where in seven, eight years we will still have a huge music industry, but not too much of a CD industry. Cutting prices like Universal did will slow the decline, but it won't stop it.

And from attorney and artist manager Ken Hertz:

Record stores don't carry nearly the inventory, in relative terms, that they once did—there aren't that many record stores, they're closing, because record companies have driven the margin out of the business. Who is going to suffer the most from the recent drop in wholesale prices by Universal? The record retailers! Because Best Buy is going to sell a $9 record for $10, but the record company is going to go from $12 down to $9, and the traditional retailers are going to go from $18 down to $10. And the artist is going to lose, and is going to bear most of the drop in price, because of the difference between an $18 retail price and a $12 retail price, in terms of a royalty . . .

Ron Stone, President of Gold Mountain Entertainment, the artist management company with Neil Young, Joni Mitchell, the Eagles, Crosby, Stills & Nash, Beck, the Foo Fighters, Sonic Youth, and the Beastie Boys as clients, comments:

I think it's the most incredibly disingenuous decision they have ever made. It reminds me of the Bush administration— it's a big lie. What they're doing is making that 25 percent cut on the back of the retailer and on the artists. That's it—they're going to make the same amount of money. Somebody figured out that they're spending more money for point and position, buying shelf space in the stores. By the way, the retailers probably make more money from the fees that they collect from the record companies than from record sales. So what Universal, being the 800 lb. gorilla that represents 38 percent of the market, they said, "Look, give us 25 percent of the shelf space, and we'll give you the price, so you could sell it at $9.99 . . . and the retailers being retailers, that's the magic bullet number— $10 a CD, that's a winner. Okay, so then they're going to make that deal—they're going to give them 25 percent of the shelf space. Then they're going to turn around to the artists, which they already are, and say, "Look, we're taking a 25–30 percent reduction in our wholesale price, and we're passing that along to you, dudes." So now they're going to make the same exact money that they started out making, and the retailer and the artists are going to take the reduction.

Singles Pricing

The sale of a "digital single" is a business model in which a music service provider such as Napster or iTunes charges the user a one-off fee of 99¢ per downloaded song. This idea has some history: the 45 RPM record was once an influential and essential promotion tool used heavily during what most would say were the heydays of rock 'n' roll. Bands like the Beatles, the Beach Boys, and the Rolling Stones all released singles on 45s as ways of distributing their tracks and kindling interest in the complete work—the LPs. Indeed the labels used to give massive quantities of singles to retailers to be sold for $.99 or $1.29 to prop up the Soundscan numbers, attract the attention of the radio program directors, and drive the songs up the charts. These days, the single has been largely phased out of the market, due to its lackluster profitability (or, shall we say, its confirmed loss-leader status), and the CD-album is pretty much the only product available to law-abiding consumers.

By essentially phasing out the single, the labels forced customers to buy CDs containing twelve or more songs in order to obtain access to the one song that they really wanted to hear. At least in economic terms, this would be okay if there was no other way of getting that single track. Along with an album, however, comes the considerable price tag that today's connected fans no longer seem to want to pay. This has certainly been one of the instrumental factors in the massive popularity of file-sharing and P2P networks—not the refusal to pay but rather the reluctance to pay the price that is being asked, for a product that is rapidly looking less attractive compared to other entertainment offerings. As a consequence, when people feel duped by the record companies, rightly so or not, they may feel equally free to "steal" from them. One could argue that record companies' refusal to adapt to technological advances and comparative pricing pressures created this "digital monster" in the first place.

The problem with track-based pricing for digital music is that it is not a good deal for anyone. It is simply a vestige of the way that music has been sold in the past: twelve songs for $12. Individual digital track pricing would have to be substantially reduced to be a good deal, and a much more "liquid" pricing system would need to be created. Sony Connect's Senior Vice President Jay Samit puts this into perspective: "The only way to make money with a 99¢ download is with corporate support," like McDonald's. "The highest-paid artist for a 99¢ download is Visa or another credit card company."

Executives at the "new" Napster and Rhapsody have a different point of view. They appear to be banking on subscription services while still providing individual track downloads on an a-la-carte basis. Sean Ryan, Real Network's Vice President of Music Services, says, "The only way to make money with a 99-cent download service is in a mix of services, including subscriptions, downloads, and radio streams. I would not want to only be an online download store at this point." Rhapsody claims to have over four hundred-fifty thousand subscribers at the time of this writing, and is offering the service directly and via ISPs Comcast and RCN. Under the terms of their subscription deal, the music is only available while the customer is online, which seems a tedious provision for most customers, and a bit early in terms of the prevailing technical infrastructure. Perhaps some form of a subscription model will really catch on in the future.

Singles, of course, have never been profitable for the recording artists, and the new pay-per-track online model being used by iTunes, Napster, Sony Connect, BuyMusic, and others are not likely to fare better. One would think that the labels could find a way to use the free tracks being distributed on the P2P networks to help promote CD sales, but no one presently seems to be thinking along those lines.

The 99-cent digital download does appear to be helping Apple to sell hardware, though, which is the primary business that Apple is in. At the time of this writing, around ten million iPods have been sold, selling in greater unit volumes than Apple's Macintosh computers, at more than 12 percent of Apple's overall revenue. Here, music is a Trojan horse for hardware, much as it has always been for the consumer electronics manufacturers. This model in which the sales of recorded music drives the sale of something else like turntables, stereos, CD players, and Walkman devices, has worked quite well for large multinational corporations such as Sony and many others. Expect to see a flood of MP3 and other digital music format players in the marketplace with more features and increasingly lower prices as hardware manufacturers take advantage of the widespread availability of digital music in the years ahead.

Compensation

The models for artist compensation need to change—and are changing. We think that the traditional approach to the label/artist business model is destined for failure, because it is not sustainable. A more equitable system might be one in which artists and their musician businesses contract directly with distributors—in most future scenarios, digital distribution services—and would take care of their marketing and production costs themselves, likely via third-party service agencies. The music service providers, in turn, could fulfill an additional marketing function by leveraging collaborative filtering and recommendation technologies, and a whole lot more.

In 2002, veteran manager Irving Azoff stated in a Reuters newswire story, "If this thing really connects, they're going to have to go back to artists and pay more of the 50/50 model than the 80/20 model they're trying to do right now." We couldn't agree more!

One of the fortunate byproducts of the current music downloading wars is the fact that the record labels are slowly but surely being forced to re-examine their contracts with artists, and the way that royalties are computed and distributed. Royalty accounting has long been the bane of artists, managers, and producers. Digital distribution is forcing the labels to move to a more transparent royalty accounting model, and this will lead to overall better compensation for artists.

Music companies and labels are also going to be looking at the overall return on investment calculations that have traditionally driven their financials. Because it is increasingly difficult to control the retail channel and drive huge hit-record successes, the labels can no longer sustain a scenario in which the one in five hundred records that sell tens of millions of units supports the records that do not sell at all. They'll also need to lower break-even points so that records do not need to sell one million copies to pay for themselves. All of this favors the small independent musician business.

Using technology to its fullest extent, the industry can achieve lower overall risk ratios. Technology can help make music more readily available to the customer and on a business-to-business level such as for films or games, and more importantly, it can also drastically lower marketing costs and other operational and administrative overhead. All of this is entirely feasible today, but requires drastic restructuring and a complete retooling of the music industry infrastructure and operating paradigms.

It remains to be seen how adept record companies will be at navigating the turbulent waters ahead; some will make it and some will not. EMI, for one, is clearly thinking about the future in fresh and creative ways. Says CFO Roger Faxon on CFO.com (February 2002):

> The record business has been focusing on the product and the product alone. But the reality is that it isn't just about the music. It's about how you get the music to consumers, how you get consumers excited about a product. It might not seem like a big leap, but the conceptual shifts are massive for our business. My view is that we must be consumer-facing. It doesn't mean that we have to be any less creative, but we have to understand how [our business] fits into the consumer context. It no longer works to say, "If we make great music, they will come."

EMI has been pioneering new business models for some time, and was one of the major labels that proactively licensed its music to the new digital distributors. EMI entered into a very creative deal with singer Robbie Williams—a deal that encompassed far more than the traditional recording contract. It also included participation in William's touring, publishing, and merchandising activities. EMI has become a partner in Robbie Williams' musician business, and is signing an increasing number of similar deals with artists in Asia and other territories. In so doing, it is helping to shape the path of profitability in the future.

Why Can't File-Sharing Be a Winner for Everybody?

Nearly seventy-five years ago, radio was threatening to destroy the existing music business. Sheet music was the "product" of the time, and people had to go to concerts to hear and see their favorite artists. Radio changed all that. According to *Music Trades* magazine, a representative of the Association of Sheet Music Dealers, Williams Arms Fisher, said at the time:

> Radio at one blow undermines the concert tours of artists who perform to potential buyers of sheet music and diverts music into the ear of those who follow the line of least resistance—by that I mean those who might desire to sing or play or perform—but with radio, content themselves by bathing in music as a pleasant sensation, and with half-hearted attention.

Amazing how shortsighted people can be when their basic interest is to preserve the status quo, rather than to embrace change. Think about what would have happened if the original large telephone companies, such as ATT and the other "Baby Bells," had insisted on a strategy of litigating the emerging cell phone players like Nextel and Cingular out of existence. What if the telephone companies had claimed the exclusive right to distribute telephone conversations? If that had happened, we might not have today's flourishing cell phone industry.

The smart move today would be for the major record labels—while they are still viable players in this business—to find a way to either appropriate or somehow license the P2P file-sharing services, in order to extract revenue from their astounding popularity. Having said that, it seems likely that they will encounter significant legal and structural hurdles that will prevent them from pulling this off without committing economic or political hara-kiri. When Cary Sherman, President of the RIAA, says, "We simply cannot allow online piracy to continue destroying the livelihoods of artists, musicians, songwriters, retailers, and everyone in the music industry," you just want to say to him: "Hey Cary, if you can't beat 'em, join 'em—or *buy 'em!*"

Just as ASCAP or BMI collect blanket licensing fees from radio stations, so could similar organizations collect blanket licensing fees from the P2P companies or ISPs, who could in turn charge the customers for access via their systems. That super-distribution model has been around since the invention of the 'Net. If 50 percent of the world's active Internet users would pay only $2 per month, the industry would collect $500 million per month—$6 billion per year—a whopping 20 percent of the current revenues from CD sales. Other calculations based on a sliding scale might work equally well, where people in developed nations paid $3–4 per month, and other emerging economies paying $1 or $0.50 or $0.25 per month to create a pool of money. And that would be just the beginning.

The record companies need to adapt to the realities of the marketplace and cast off their antiquated business models, just like they have cast off the thousands of artists whose records did not sell enough copies of their first album. Legitimate music distribution businesses can outdo the existing "rogue" P2P networks by developing their own delivery and customer interaction systems that employ superior technologies, recommendation engines, and customer service—watch for this to happen eventually.

In fact, Napster's founder Shawn Fanning is quietly working with the record companies on a project called "Snocap" to create a way of filtering and tracking P2P file-sharing. By identifying files via a "fingerprint" and comparing the file to its database, the Snocap software could, in theory, provide a payment mechanism for files traded via peer-to-peer networks. Such a concept should be very appealing to current content "owners" who wish to maintain control over their property, but not likely very appealing to the P2P companies who may wish to develop more enlightened business models. It remains to be seen whether the record labels will or will not agree to do business with their former nemeses. For now, many of these companies (and people) are simply blacklisted, and anyone who wants to do business with the labels has to stay away from them.

New Operating Mantras

Without sounding too "California," we believe that more relevant and more mindful music business models of the future must be based on the following paradigms:

Respect. There must be respect for the underlying intent of the original copyright principles, a healthy balance of the creator's rights versus the user's rights, and dedication to upholding fair-use and first-sale doctrines.

Sharing. Music should be shareable among its audiences. Whether the process includes the sharing of the actual media files or not is less relevant than the sustainability of communities that share their music.

Portability. People are increasingly mobile, thus digital music needs to be mobile and "un-wired."

Transparency. All parties involved (i.e., the consumer, the provider, and the creator) must strive to create and maintain a mutual understanding in regards to how the proceeds are to be split up and distributed. Transparency is the key.

Fair Pricing. Music products and services need to be market driven and priced according to their actual market value at any given time, in relation to location, timing, level of access, user rights, and comparative value with other media.

Easy Access to Music. Everything should always be available, at any location, and playable on any device.

Without true, no-frills, no-parachute cooperation, and serious compromises on the part of the current music business players, a fair, equitable, and *timely* solution to the current music industry crisis will be difficult to achieve. Therefore, we may still have to go through something like a systematic marketplace failure that may be difficult to recover from without outside (i.e., non-government) intervention.

New Licensing Approaches

One solution may be the introduction of some kind of a license that all record labels either would or must grant, by default, to any legitimate online music retailers. Another option is to institute a small fee in the form of a "utility license" or—dare we say it—tax that would allow people to download any and all music online. This fee could be included in the price of blank media, MP3 players, ISPs, DSL, wireless, and cable.

If the involved industries cannot voluntarily agree on and create such a legal structure themselves—and do so soon—then maybe the governments should do it, as happened several times before, such as with radio in the 1920s and cable television in the 1970s. Community antenna television, now called cable television, was started by John and Margaret Watson in 1948, in Pennsylvania. They set up an antenna on a local mountaintop, and received clear broadcast signals from the three Pennsylvania stations. The antenna was then connected to Watson's store via a cable and modified signal boosters. Watson later connected the mountain antenna to both his store and several of his clients' homes that were located along the cable path—the first CATV system in history.

When cable television operators first re-used the freely available "on-air" television feeds and plugged them into their cable systems, the large television networks sued them over the use of their programs, and the ensuing litigation went on to the U.S. Supreme Court. The U.S. Congress finally decreed a compulsory license. In 1976, U.S. Congress passed the Copyright Revision Act, which established a "compulsory license," allowing cable systems to retransmit broadcast stations. It also set fee schedules for carrying distant signals for the first time, making the cable operator also responsible for copyright payments (17 U.S.C. 101-118). In 1970, about 7 percent of homes had cable television (Donnerstein, 1994), but today everyone has it—more revenues for all involved parties, but years of struggle to make it happen. Technology prevailed but it took the legal system a few decades to catch up.

Government involvement may actually be necessary to address and solve the anti-trust implications of any widespread, cross-industry collaboration among the major players, without whom significant momentum would be unattainable. As they have done before, perhaps the U.S. Congress, or indeed the European Commission, can chisel out a fair and equitable solution that supports the needs and desires of all parties: writers, musicians, labels, publishers, and consumers alike. This would make more sense than trying to preserve and support a monopoly that is quickly becoming outmoded.

Terry Fischer, Harvard professor and author of *Promises to Keep* (Stanford University Press, 2004), has proposed an Alternative Compensation System for the music and media business. He suggests either a compulsory system funded through user fees or taxes and managed by government agencies, or a voluntary system funded by subscription fees and based around an entertainment co-op model. In either case, authors are compensated from a large pool of money based on the relative popularity of the author's work across the system. Artists would have to register their work with the copyright office or another agency, which would track usage and collect the fees. Professor Fischer said that he is working with the Brazilian Minister of Culture, musician Gilberto Gil, to explore this idea. A very descriptive chapter from his book is available at cyber.law.harvard.edu/people/tfisher/PTKChapter6.pdf.

Fisher is one of a handful of pioneers, including Lawrence Lessig and his Creative Commons venture, who are exploring the potential of fair use, copyright, and media in the twenty-first century. You can read more about some of these initiatives at the Berkman Center for Internet and Society at Harvard University and their Digital Media Project at cyber.law.harvard.edu/media/overview.

The 'Net has already become the leading "information utility" for a good many people; licensing content as part of this utility is just the next step. The Electronic Frontier Foundation (www.eff.org), one of the leading think tanks in this area and advocates of civil liberty, describes two licensing alternatives: voluntary collective licensing and compulsory licensing. Here are their models, explained.

Voluntary Collective Licensing: Copyright holders could join together and voluntarily offer blanket licenses. This solution does not require any changes to the current copyright law and leaves the price-setting to the copyright owners. This approach has been used in radio and broadcast licensing for the past seventy years, and performing rights organizations were formed to administer it. In the U.S., ASCAP, BMI, and SESAC have been collecting fees from the radio and television stations ever since, passing the monies on to the publishers and writers. Their European equivalents also work hand-in-hand with yet other societies such as the PPL (U.K.) and the GVL (Germany), which collect money on behalf of the performing artists and the owner of the recording, an idea that is making only slow progress in the U.S.

The record companies and music publishers could proceed to implement such a system, without having to change any applicable laws. Back in 2001, the "old," ill-fated Napster offered $1 billion to agree to this idea, and was turned down. Sharman Networks, owner of the popular Kazaa P2P network, and the newly founded P2P United Foundation in Washington, D.C., have undertaken similar efforts and are now lobbying both in Washington and Brussels to get the attention of lawmakers. The seemingly insurmountable problem is that virtually all rights owners and their stakeholders would need to agree to this licensing procedure, and therefore enjoin and forego the usual barrage of lawsuits, in exchange for a reasonable piece of the pie—an unprecedented assumption. Not surprisingly, so far, the big entertainment companies have shown no interest in pursuing a voluntary collective licensing plan.

A voluntary collective license for music on digital networks, if drafted with great care, may solve these problems by simply creating a large "pool of money" generated by online file trading, and then determining a fair way to split it up. While the record companies and the publishers have had ample opportunity to voluntarily put such a licensing system in place, making it easy for consumers to get the music that they want digitally, it is quite unlikely that they will ever do so of their own accord, for what is now a familiar reason: they lose control. But as Jim Griffin puts it quite succinctly, "Every time we exercise control, we lose. Every time we let go, the thing we fought becomes the thing that feeds us. We need a way to monetize the anarchy."

Historically, voluntary licensing has rarely been the solution to adapting to massive discontinuities in the way business is done, because it severely threatens the existing status quo, the distribution of cash, and the incumbent power structures.

Compulsory Licensing: Compulsory licensing has been proven necessary in the case of player pianos, cable television, satellite television, digital recording media, and Internet radio, and it appears to have served the respective constituents well. Compulsory licenses are used to legally allow music to be played on the radio, in restaurants, stores, elevators, and in shopping malls as background music. When copyright holders can't reach consensus on licensing terms, Congress has properly stepped forward and required them to adhere to the rules it stipulated. The very first compulsory license in the U.S. (1909) targeted player pianos, allowing the so-called "mechanical" reproduction of other people's songs. Today, this license forms the underpinnings of the most stable and reliable form of payment to songwriters, the "mechanical royalty."

One way to collect a pool of money would be to get the ISPs to add a small monthly fee to their current charges in order to include digital music services. This is being looked into in Europe, e.g., with a company called Play Louder ISP. This fee would be passed on to the rights holders (artists/writers, publishers, and labels), therefore essentially taxing the bandwidth used to deliver the music. Another part of the solution would be an additional levy or sales tax on digital media and media players such as CDRs, iPods, and CD burners. Some combination of these methods could be used to establish that ominous "pool of money." Then, a fair and transparent way to split it up and distribute it would need to be devised—perhaps a good task for today's performing rights organizations (PRO) and mechanical rights organizations (MROs).

This "content tax" seems like a reasonable solution to the current, rather ridiculous environment in which each piece of music must be individually licensed, from each rights owner, on a track-by-track basis. This new tax could be a form of insurance against online piracy, and rather than trying to sue everyone to force an overall change in consumer attitudes and behavior, the industry would simply "tax" them.

This would let consumers make unlimited copies of the songs in whatever forms they wished, and would allow them to legally share and discover music together, without the need for secret and private "darknets" that allow member-only access, or the fear of lawsuits by the recording industry. The users would pay only slightly more for their Internet services, blank media, and consumer electronics, but the music would feel like free.

It would seem plausible that two pools could be created: one to compensate the publishers and writers, and another to compensate the labels and the recording artists. These pools would be split 50/50 between the label and artist, and the publisher and writer. Such an approach may cut through the legal issues involved in artist and publishing contracts, and would seem like a fair way to compensate everyone.

We believe that charging for music at the primary point of access, rather than in every single instance, is a powerful concept—similar to the utility model used by water and power companies. This certainly makes the transaction easier for the customer, and creates transparency and liquidity. Most consumers already get their monthly bills from their ISPs, phone companies, or other utility companies, and anyone using the account could access the music, thus solving the many issues related to who has a credit card and who does not. It seems that an unprecedented opportunity exists for the music industry to solve the online piracy problem, by working with the government and digital network providers.

On a per-person basis, the fee that would need to be charged is actually quite small. The International Federation of the Phonographic Industry reports U.S. gross revenue for 2002 to be $12.3 billion. With current estimates at approximately 167 million people online in the U.S., that would amount to about $6 per month, per person, using gross dollars—but as outlined above, that would assume a total displacement of the revenues derived from the sale of CDs. That is highly unlikely in the next ten to fifteen years, if indeed it will ever occur. And if we were to look at the numbers another way and consider the "street value," i.e. what people actually pay for CDs, and divide it by the total number of people who purchase music, the figure would more like $2–$3 per person online, per month. Again, if one allows for the many up-selling and cross-selling opportunities that could additionally be exploited, even $1 per month may work, and would certainly represent a fantastic value to the music fan. Imagine total ubiquity for the price of a bus token!

If the record companies and publishers were to be compelled to license at least a large majority of their catalogs (and archives!) in this manner, we believe it could nearly double their profits, because they would still profit from the CD sales that are likely to continue for some time, albeit of course with a downward trend. And let's keep in mind that this "new" money would be extremely profitable because it is pure licensing income for everyone, and few additional costs would need to be incurred.

This argument should not be lost on today's artists and writers: licensing fees can be split more or less evenly, resulting in a much better deal for artists and writers alike, way beyond what they are currently getting from the sales of recorded music, if they are getting anything at all. A scheme like this would make online music legitimate, create a huge and growing pool of cash to compensate everyone involved, and give the music industry enough time to retool its business models.

A Digital Utility License for Media Companies

The future of music will be most significantly influenced by those who can give their customers a completely integrated and cross-marketed mix of recorded music, live shows, merchandising, tickets, artist access, mobile music, video games, television, radio, film, software, and other publishing and information products. Integrating music purchasing and enjoyment into an overall entertainment or lifestyle experience is a model that may work very well. Similar to cable television, in which you pay for a package of services, music can be buried into a larger package. Who can do this? In the U.S., AOL, MSN, Yahoo, MTV (Viacom), Sony, cable television networks, and others like them. But will they?

When cable television reared its head, the broadcast and television networks fought it tooth and nail. In the absence of any clear regulations in this field, CATV operators started to rebroadcast copyrighted programming to a willing public of what would nowadays be called "pirates," until the unresolved complaints and actions of the copyright owners forced Congress to step in and solve the problem, to the ultimate benefit of all. There clearly was a desire and need on the part of the consumer, demonstrated by a willingness to pirate the signals. There was also a need for an improved and efficient system for distributing the shows at higher quality levels and to a more geographically diverse population than prior broadcast systems could address. The combination of market demand and technological superiority appeared unstoppable. Sound familiar?

Well, let's see what happened subsequently, and find the lesson here. A vastly expanded broadcast and production industry was allowed to develop, creating cash, jobs, and opportunities for people, companies, and cities around the world. Entirely new concepts, such as "superstations" and PPV channels, were developed along with a thousand niche channels programmed to address the needs of sports fans, movie buffs, news addicts, and many other interest areas.

Production companies flourished, as did the distributors. Advertising revenues grew alongside entirely new revenue streams based on subscriptions and pay-per-view events. More actors, musicians, set designers, producers, makeup artists, camera operators, technicians, booking agents, and hundreds of related professionals could find jobs than ever before. Radical transformation gave way to unprecedented growth and opportunity, once the incumbent media moguls were forced to play the new game that their customers demanded.

A New Type of Music Company

Here is a framework for a new music business model for a "next-generation" music company—one that is fully aligned and synchronized with the interests of the artist and fan. We see some of this already emerging, most notably with the Sanctuary Group, management companies like The Firm, and organizations such as the IMMF already heading down this path. We believe that the music company of the future will be active in a number of things, including artist management, publishing, touring, merchandising, and recording. The *artists'* brands will drive the business, and the win-win-win economics between artist, company, and fan will make the risk more tolerable and the return on investment more predictable. Instead of betting on a traditional 10-to-1 recording model that relies on huge CD sales from just a few artists, the now-evolving business model can test-market artists more efficiently, and work on much lower volumes by spreading the risk across multiple revenue streams and different forms of "product."

For example, building artists as brands requires a constant release of energy into the marketplace. Using the digital networks to distribute the music, bundles of two to three songs can be released to test the waters, not unlike the old "singles" business or, more recently, the "EP" business. Rather than investing in the production of a complete album at first, the company can continuously release music into the marketplace, and the songs can be used to support the tours and keep the music fresh and the company nimble. A more rational, slower-growth approach can be used to support multiple artists with less financial risk—versus the "bet the farm" mentality of the old record business.

This new musician-business model combines the functions of a record label, management company, publisher, and merchandiser into a single entity or related set of entities, such as the Sanctuary Group. The company signs artists to deals in which the artists retain ownership of the masters, and only license (lease) them to the company for a limited time. Artists create their own recordings, and the company takes this music to market in digital and hard formats, creates merchandise to sell, and provides management and touring logistics for live performances. The company also acts as the publisher for all songs written while under contract. This increases the potential return on investment for each artist signed, by aligning the interests of the artist, manager, label, and publisher into a single entity that splits all of the revenue streams. This model is based on lowering the cost of production, distribution, and promotion for all parties to minimize the risk of financing a new act—and maximizing potential return.

The skills that are essential to recognizing talent, helping to develop that talent, and matching artists with potentially receptive audiences are at the heart of the game—both in the record business of the past and in the musician business of the future. But by marrying this effort with all the revenue streams available to an artist, a broadly defined musician business can reduce its risks and lower the break-even point of the overall investment. The potential conflicts of interest that can arise from having artist management inside of the overall revenue generating engine can be minimized to a degree by keeping the term of the artist's contract reasonably short and the financial accounting transparent.

This model is not unlike what EMI has done with Robbie Williams or the model that bands like Phish and String Cheese Incident are already using within their own companies, and similar to the model of an independent record label with a publishing arm. The major change is the integration of management and touring into the business mix. This way, the company can take an integrated and synchronized marketing approach across all the revenue possibilities and try to maximize income and opportunity.

We think this model is particularly interesting in light of the negative effects of unlicensed music distribution via P2P networks on recording and mechanical income. By maximizing the revenue potential by including touring, publishing, and merchandising in the mix, the company can try new creative marketing approaches that leverage freely (and cheaply) distributed music to drive other income streams.

As Seth Rosen wrote in *U.S. News & World Report*, "Ultimately the creative industries may have to adapt to a new role in which they act more as publicists and less as distributors, perhaps earning a percentage of the artist's revenues."

How Technology Will Rewire the Music Business

I f technology has all this positive potential for the music business, why is all of this taking so darn long? Why does it seem
that so few people are actually doing the really obvious things
that could be done to turn the music business around? Why did
the first wave of digital music end up as a mere drop in the bucket?

The simple answer lies in the sheer conviction to resist transformative change, the macho-dinosaurian attitudes, and the country-
club networks that still prevail in many areas of the music industry.
From the invention of the gramophone to the advent of electric and
electronic instruments, to the recordable cassette tape and the digital
compact disc, the music industry has always made a big leap in size,
revenues, and profits when the next wave of technology hit home.
But not always voluntarily.

Just about every new transformative technology was fought,
tooth and nail, until it could no longer be contained, discredited, or
sued out of existence, and only *then* it was reluctantly embraced, its
providers acquired and controlled, then put to work to bring in the
bacon. The cacophonous endless loop of the music industry innovation cycle goes something like this: ignore it → discredit it → stomp it
out → litigate against it → attempt to reverse engineer/copy it → buy
a piece of it → own it → start all over again.

By some tacit rule, this is the way it has been since the invention of the gramophone—except this time, at the dawn of the
much-lauded "economy of knowledge and emotion," this change is
powered by zeroes and ones. The stakes are much higher, the ship is
so much bigger, the tides are surging so much stronger, the cliffs are
huge, and the wind is blowing harder. This time, the ship may need
to actually capsize before a new course can be set. Socrates said,
"Only the extremely ignorant or the extremely intelligent can resist
change," and if that wisdom were to be put to test here, one cannot
ignore history. Utterly intelligent or utterly ignorant? Take a guess.

Radio was stamped as stealing and "unfettered thievery" by the
music publishers, and the first radio operators were unanimously
hated by the "industry." Sound familiar? In 1914, the American Society
of Composers, Authors and Publishers (ASCAP) was formed—in direct
response to that deadly threat of radio—to represent composers'
rights. It sued radio stations to enforce the copyrights of its members,
after unsuccessfully attempting to negotiate licenses directly with the

radio stations. Needless to say, neither party could settle on a deal, until finally the U.S. Congress stepped in and prescribed a statutory license. Ditto for cable television, and the VCR, and for tape-levies in Europe. The ASCAP lawsuits had a surprisingly similar tone as the RIAA lawsuits have today; however, eventually the Supreme Court ruled that the radio stations were *not* in violation of copyright but in fact had to only compensate ASCAP and its members for the use of their copyrighted material. Thus, the broadcast license was born—via legislation.

When re-recordable tapes were injected into the mainstream, the record companies again tried to litigate to prevent this new format from entering the market. They argued that recordable tape in the hands of the consumer, and thus millions of part-time pirates, would ruin the industry. RIAA president at the time, Stan Gortikov, mused, "For every album sold, one is taped. In our henhouse, poachers now almost outnumber the chickens." This rhetoric sounds so familiar—so little learned in forty years?

Whether it was radio in the 1920s, cassette recorders in the 1960s, or digital music in the 1990s, the industry reaction has always been the same—but the outcomes have almost always been the same, too. As the power shifts from the old technology towards the new transformative technologies, from sheet music publishers in the very early days of the music business, to record producers thereafter, from live performances to radio, very few business sectors vanished completely. The market just got bigger, all around. In most cases, though—and this is what is happening to the audio CD—innovation drives the prices of yesterday's technologies into the dirt. Following the broad adoption of legal digital alternatives, we can expect that to happen with music prices, as well.

In the end, no legal rule, whether subject to a great amount of government lobbying or not, is strong enough to overcome a radical technical innovation. Rather, legal rules that go against the actual habits of millions of people tend to be adapted eventually. The courts may delay the inevitable progress but they cannot stop it. This is why CD prices are bound to be drastically reduced, while the digital music experience unfolds. Radio became the lubricant that drove massive record sales beyond the wildest expectations of the record companies. We owe the impressive expansion of music sales in the past seventy years in no small part to the invention of radio, and ultimately to the compulsory licenses that allowed radio companies to operate and flourish.

Technology has always driven the entertainment industries, and it will do so again, in a digitally networked society.

Historical Perspectives

The invention and standard-setting establishment of the 12-tone "tempered" piano three hundred years ago facilitated the use of a standardized, universal instrument throughout Western civilization. When piano notation was invented, people gained a method of writing down their songs so that they could remember every single note from a specific performance, and others could replicate that performance without ever actually having heard it performed. The player piano took music technology up another big step: combining the performer and the "machine" in a free-standing audio output. Player pianos powered by humans were the first form of "reproduced" music.

When electricity came around in the late nineteenth century, everything changed again. Electricity is, of course, the major stepping-stone to the machine-driven age that was waiting around the corner, in the twentieth century. Electricity has made people extremely powerful, yet also extremely dependent—a bit of a twisted duality that seems to surface repeatedly. Electricity enabled the development of sophisticated music technology such as recording and amplification, two milestones in today's entire music business culture. Recording technologies allowed for mass distribution of any kind of music, anywhere, and also changed the kind of music that was created. Songs were shortened to fit the format and were fixed in time, forever to be duplicated and repeated exactly the same way every time. Amplification allowed for big shows and gigantic concert tours to take place, enabling musicians to reach out to large audiences, and creating the multi-billion-dollar concert industry that we know today. Radio enabled new music to be broadcast and heard all around the globe, and played a major part in creating a more musically ubiquitous society. A much larger audience. Ubiquitous media. Omnipresent music—and more money for all involved.

As personal computers became smaller and yet more powerful, digital files became more widely used by the production people in the music industry, in an effort to lower the costs of recording and editing procedures. Computers and music producers were friends, from the very first days of the Altair and the Sinclair. Computers drove the MIDI sequencer and changed the recording and editing process, and by recording multitrack MIDI and digital audio files, music producers could create intricate recordings, develop any musical texture imaginable, and later on edit just about any aspect of the sound. The birth of the compact disc propelled digital music into the mainstream, and the digital file is smack dab in the middle of the current file-sharing debate.

As with many previous technologies, it can be argued that P2P networks today are expanding consumers' experiences with music to yet another, higher level. Just as the industry ultimately benefited financially from radio, the cassette, and other disruptive technologies, the industry will certainly find a way to financially benefit from P2P—it is inevitable.

Technology in the Hands of Artists

Digital technologies such as CDs, personal computers, digital recorders, signal processors, and the Internet have already radically transformed the music business. Unless you are performing music live on acoustic instruments and singing without the aid of amplification, there is very little you can do in music today that is not impacted dramatically by technology. It has made music easier and cheaper to produce, record, edit, mix, duplicate, distribute, and promote. Indeed, the recording engineers and producers, and the musicians themselves, have driven much of the transformation.

Today, it is entirely possible for musicians to write, arrange, record, and master albums on CD in the comfort of their own home studios, at a cost often less than $5,000, including all the equipment and software. That is not to say that the quality will be the same as if they had recorded a professionally produced CD in a $250,000 recording studio, but one thing is for sure: the threshold has been lowered, and just about anyone can produce their own CD.

This fact has wreaked havoc on the recording studio business, as most artists no longer need to spend a fortune renting elaborate facilities for recording, editing, and mixing. Of course, many still do make their records in high-end recording facilities, more often than not at the request of the record label that is backing them. But the vast majority of music being recorded today is being done on a low budget, utilizing digital technologies that put control into the hands of the creatives rather than the bookkeepers. In a way, digital technologies have democratized this process, but they also have injected a good deal of Darwinism into the business. The more people record, produce, and publish their works, the more new releases will vie for our attention. And today, getting attention is the name of the game.

Software products such as Pro Tools, Reason, Live, Sonor, Performer, and Acid have become very popular tools for music makers. Pro Tools, for example, has 85 percent market share in the U.S., and is an application that models all the features of a traditional multitrack recording studio, running on a personal computer. The program features a wide range of studio capabilities, from editing to mixing to very advanced signal processing, all at a much lower cost than its traditional recording counterpart. Reason is a program that simulates the signal processing and functionality of a vast array of hardware devices. Software is now fully integrated in the music creation process—in the home studio, the laptop sits right next to the acoustic guitar.

Along with the advent of the personal computer as a recording and "artistic" device came a new dependence on the digital file formats. Digital files are transferred, manipulated, corrupted, watermarked, watched, listened to, and lost. We can read, write, upload, and download whatever kind of music we want, in any digital file format. What used to be prohibitively expensive technology is now a common, mass-market technology—and it took less than twenty years.

It was the music engineers that discovered a way to take the digital files contained on a music CD and transfer them onto a personal computer. This was driven by the desire to transfer and sample music. Engineers have also driven the development of file-compression technologies, such as MP3. The MP3 format flourished in part because it minimized file size while maintaining the perceived quality of the original digital recording. One thing leads to another. . . .

From the angle of music production, music software programs like Acid, Reason, and Live make new music by combining lots of "raw" pre-made material, including sound bites, samples, and loops that musicians can combine in any way they want to. All that is left is for the artist to do is to put the song components together and create their own personalized music. This "cut-and-paste artistry" has fueled the production of hip-hop, dance, techno, and many modern genres. One can argue about the relative musicianship required to create and remix music using these new software tools—but there is no arguing over the popularity of this new music.

There is no doubt that ubiquitous music production software that brings with it the ease of recording, mixing, and editing, combined with the ability to effortlessly distribute music online, is playing a role in propelling the music business into the twenty-first century. Once again, the pie gets better—more options and bigger markets.

The Ravages of Free

We believe that music has always been obtained for what feels like free. Many performances are seemingly free, radio is free, music television is free, tapes from my friends were free, music from the library was free . . . and CDs have always been sold piggy-backing on a tacit "up-sell" tactic: you liked what you heard somewhere else, you discovered it, you checked it out, and sooner or later you actually paid money for it. Interest turns into exploration, which turns into buying something, which might turn into a relationship.

Check out this quote by L.A.-based music attorney Ken Hertz:

When you buy a seat at a concert you don't pay for the music. Everybody gets the same music—you pay for the seat. You pay to be closer to the stage. The guy in the front row pays $500 while the guy in the back row pays $10. Why? They both get exactly the same concert. They're not paying for the music; they're paying for the experience. They want to brag about it, they want to talk about it; they want the memory of it. But it has nothing to do with the music. In fact, when they leave, they are music-free. They didn't get to keep any of the music that they just paid all that money to experience.

We believe that "paying for the experience" will be the prime paradigm behind the pricing of music going forward—a complete turnaround from the fixed value paradigms of "mechanical reproductions" and CD prices.

Unstoppable P2P File-Sharing

Of course, the real question is how the content industries can monetize the consumer's conduct, not how the increasing criminalization of the alleged perpetrators can be best achieved. This very thought has been proven wrong, time and time again. Consider the debate on the legalization of marijuana, where it is now becoming obvious that criminalizing tens of millions of people for a widely tolerated behavior does not produce any positive results for society at large.

Reports find that large and increasing percentages of Americans already download music regularly, followed closely by the British, the Germans, and the Danish, as well as the Japanese. Depending on which report you believe—and there are many opposing metrics being offered—as many as half of the downloaders that were questioned report that they are buying fewer CDs as a result of their downloading activities. No doubt, people are getting used to handling music digitally, and it will be only a few years before the majority of the music-loving public will be getting it digitally, one way or the other.

Forrester Research analysts, for one, predict that physical media like CDs and DVDs will soon become obsolete as consumers multi-access entertainment through computers, cell phones, WiFi, PDAs, and other portable devices. And let's keep in mind that it's not just P2P networks that are the purveyors of those goodies—files are also being traded via an increasingly varied and sophisticated array of other new technologies. Long before Napster was conceived, files were already being traded on IRC (Internet Relay Chat) via UseNet groups, and on "private" FTP sites. Social networking sites such as Friendster are entering that fray, as well. Down the road, we may very well find networking, Friendster-type meeting sites, and dating sites turning into playlist and file-swapping platforms.

Files are also traded via instant messaging, another form of P2P networking on which it is very difficult to track the individual messages. Add to these methods the exploding phenomena of dark-nets—newly revitalized member-only networks and P2P Web clubs that are being formed by sophisticated geeks and Web-nerds in order to prevent network-based snooping by unauthorized third parties. Darknets make it possible for their members to trade any kind of data or information anonymously. The file-sharing phenomenon is quite certainly beyond anybody's ability to effectively regulate or control. The rush into criminalization has only served to push the sophisticated users into the cover of darkness—a pyrrhic victory, if you ever saw one.

The Single Largest Market on the Planet

At the time of this writing, over seventy-two million people are esti-mated to be downloading music via the various file-sharing networks in the U.S., and more than five hundred million people have down-loaded the Kazaa software—and there are many other P2P systems like it. Around ten million P2P users are online at any given moment, and this number is growing every day.

As a "*community of pirates,*" as the RIAA has taken to calling them, these music fans represent the largest music market on the planet. Is this phenomenon just going to disappear? As Fred von Lohmann of the Electronic Frontier Foundation said about the 2003 RIAA lawsuits, "Trying to throw sixty million Americans in jail is not a reasonable approach. That's more than voted for President Bush [in 2000]."

Why can we not just monetize this conduct? Can't something that is practiced so widely become the starting ramp for a legitimate business? At this rate of denial, the ever-expanding market for unau-thorized music sharing will continue to outstrip the industry's own fledgling online music services, perhaps forever. At the time of this writing, an estimated three billion songs are being downloaded ille-gally each month, and more music is being traded online every day. This is a force that has to be reckoned with if the (ex-record) music companies are to survive.

What's more, in the court of public opinion, the record compa-nies have long lost their case against the omnipresent file-sharers, a defeat that cannot be underestimated in terms of loss of customer trust. To regain the customers' trust, the coming digital music industry, the next generation of the music business, will need to work extra hard to provide a lot of added values in order to earn back the respect of music fans. The strategy of criminalization—"downloading is a crime"—is no more likely to work today for the record business than it did a century ago, when the leading automobile manufacturers tried to squelch the threat of cheap, mass-produced cars by suing consumers who bought Henry Ford's automobiles. Or, for that matter, it may be as effective as labeling a cigarette box with a huge label that says, "CIGARETTE SMOKING KILLS." Do you know any smoker that pays attention to those labels?

Chris Evans, founder of Internet Freedom (www.netfreedom.org), said:

> The recording industry is attempting to take the moral high ground by making out that it represents the true interests of artists. The reality is that for decades they have exploited artists and fixed prices. Instead of embracing new technology and new models of distribution, the recording industry has finally woken up to a world to which it no longer belongs. Suing Napster makes as much sense as suing a blank cassette tape. Rather than trying to put twenty million Napster users in the dock, the recording industry would be wiser to end its anti-progressive practices and work to develop new models of distribution which benefit artists and fans alike.

The bottom line is that technology can be and will be used to "put Humpty together again," and that is all that there is to it!

The Digital Chastity Belt

As part of the anti-circumvention provisions of the now infamous Digital Millennium Copyright Act (DMCA), major technology providers have been developing new digital rights management (DRM) schemes for the past decade. These high-tech methods of protecting copyrighted material include the use of digital "wrappers" that prevent access to the file under certain rules, the use of encryption, software keys, and digital watermarking/fingerprinting. These methods would further restrict access to digital content and, according to the doctrine, prevent unauthorized copying.

Unfortunately, to date there has been no DRM that does not also infringe on fair-use doctrines, such as the right to resell a CD and the right to make a limited number of private copies. Music consumers in a digital society will undoubtedly reject any limitations on the actual use of their music. Why would you accept new limitations in the face of more powerful, inexpensive, and efficient technologies that are geared to provide you with more benefits rather than fewer?

No surprises: the consumer pretty much hates the very idea of DRM, while Hollywood and Big Music have wet dreams about it, and the technology and hardware companies are stuck in the middle.

You may already be familiar with some types of DRM. For example, some DVDs will only work in designated players, a fact that we find to be evidence of an appalling disregard for the customer's rights. U.S.-purchased DVDs will often not play in machines in Europe; this is already an utterly unacceptable limitation of the consumer's rights, and will certainly not lead people to buy more DVDs once they can easily download movies via the Internet. It seems like this old style of doing business ("prevent people from doing x-y-z so that they need to give us more money to get what they want") should already be abolished. On the contrary, it is kept alive and well in the entertainment business, particularly in music.

A lot of music editing and production software that we have described is copy protected, requiring hardware keys or elaborate installation and authorization schemes in order to fully operate the software. While this is frequently circumvented, with certain Internet sites offering the latest software codes to anyone that cares to find them, preventing the easy copying of professional-grade software products is very different than preventing consumers from having a great and simple experience when they want to watch movies or listen to music.

DRM has become a much-disputed, central piece of the puzzle in the industry's ongoing efforts to prevent piracy, both online as well as offline. Technologies involving watermarking and assigning DRM wrappers to songs have been considered, tried, and employed in some instances. A leader in video and DVD encryption, Macrovision, is moving aggressively into the music market, but so far most trials with copy-protected CDs have backfired. Many consumers have started to reject CDs that are limited in this way; there have even been lawsuits from some consumers in Germany.

Watermarking is another approach designed to inject account-ability into the end-user scenario. Watermarking is the process of encrypting additional data onto a digital music file that, in theory, would allow the industry to use a simple scan procedure to find out where a copy of any given song originated, and therefore potentially identify the person responsible for its illegal or unauthorized dissemi-nation. Pioneered by Musicode (now Verance), watermarking is inau-dible to the average ear. The primary purpose of a watermark is to track the use of a song, rather than to proactively prevent its dissemination. It has very powerful implications for performance royalty administra-tion and, potentially, the identification of illegal distributors.

Interestingly, watermarks also add another layer of account-ability to the mix. With a watermarked file or signal, you can still distribute any given track to anyone else, but now your personal ID will be engraved on it, as well. In a way, you are broadcasting your involvement for anyone that would care to take a look. Having said that, it is quite clear that watermarks can be removed or made inef-fective by knowledgeable people inclined to do so, and many water-marking "hacks" are available on the Internet—like all technology, countermeasures will always be feasible if adequate resources are put behind it.

Ultimately, there is no strictly *technological* solution that can allow the user the full and unrestricted use of content while also maintaining an effective level of control by the creator, owner, or legal representative of the content, since any good technology will always impact and change the underlying business paradigms, as well. This dilemma started the day that computing was invented, and very likely, it can only be solved by some careful and smart economic and/or social engineering—by means of price, value, and ethics.

In the summer of 2003, BMG released a copy-protected disc on its Arista label. The much-lauded protection scheme, supplied by Macrovision archrival SunnCom, was easily cracked by a Princ-eton University student within days. The student was subsequently sued by BMG. The "hack" was simply to hold down the shift key on a Windows PC while loading the disc into the computer, and the CD would be easily copyable. A similar situation occurred earlier that year when Sony released a copy-protected disc that could be defeated by drawing around the edge of the disc with a permanent felt-tipped marker. There is no end to human ingenuity and there is always a way to get that chastity belt off, thank goodness.

From a marketing standpoint, however, some of the technologies that are used to copy-protect CDs also could allow for the inclusion of so-called "second-session" content that the consumer could access via a PC. This content could take the form of "CD Extra" or enhanced CDs, and would include bonus items such as images, biographies, and the like. The idea would be to give the consumer a few extra items in exchange for his acceptance of the anti-copying provisions—throw in a few jpegs and video clips in exchange for tethering the file to that little piece of plastic, forever. While offering additional multimedia content is a very good idea, this approach has proved to be fundamentally flawed since it is highly unlikely that any customer would want to quickly forego his fair-use rights in such a manner, for such fluff.

Indeed, the latest move in this turf saw SunnCom striking a deal with Microsoft to use Windows Media 9 technology to allow the customer to copy the tracks onto a PC, but not to upload and trade them on the Internet. What if I want to digitize the track to go onto my car library, my MP3 player, or my shower?

DRM's goal is to combat digital piracy and to deter file-sharing activities. However, we believe that it directly conflicts with the fair-use traditions that are, albeit without significant legal anchoring, ingrained in what people have come to consider "common law."

With the Digital Millennium Copyright Act and the respective mindsets at the roots of its adoption, the copyright holders seem to be gaining increasing control. The penalties for circumventing copy-protection measures are high, yet there is no clear definition of what exactly the law does apply to—a carte blanche for content monopolies?

DRM appears to be a significant part of the strategy for the major record labels that remain intent on squeezing every last possible nickel out of the old business model through consolidation, belt-tightening, and reorganization. Charles Goldstuck, President and COO for BMG North America, laid out the agenda for BMG for 2005 during his keynote speech at the New York Plug-In Conference. The priorities at BMG are to focus on combating piracy through legal means, pressure Congress to force publishers toward compulsory rates (as long as such

Music Recommendation

Smart software and music-specific search engines will replace the good old radio as the primary way that people learn about new music. When all the music ever recorded can fit on a hard drive costing less that $400—when there is more free music available than you could ever listen to in a lifetime—the name of the game will be finding the music that you like.

One cannot overestimate the importance of music recommendation, playlist-sharing, collaborative filtering, and agenting schemes. Thousands of music-marketing experts have tried to crack this nut in the offline world, from record reviews to MTV, but now digital technologies will finally put this Holy Grail into reach. In a future where all content is quickly available on digital networks, it will simply be easier to employ viral and vastly exponential ways of reaching a music fan who may be a good match with any given artist.

Software, when coupled with the superdistribution power of a digital network, can make it much easier for people to find highly relevant music than ever before, whether it's a new release or a track that sat in some archive in India for the past thirty-five years. In addition to the good old and trusted Western purveyors of such information, such as *Rolling Stone, Village Voice, Vibe, Mojo, Spin, NME,* and many others, people are increasingly turning to the Web for new music reviews, recommendations, and leads.

And we don't mean just *publishing information* about new music, but actually proactively and with high accuracy *steering* you to music that you will very likely enjoy because of your previous listening patterns, download or CD orders, membership in peer groups, concert ticket purchases—in short, because of your lifestyle and *because of who you are*. This, of course, gives rise to concerns of privacy and personal data security.

Some existing technologies, such as MusicGenome, can actually recommend musical works that are outside of the genres that you usually listen to, so that not all recommendations would be jazz tracks just because you listen to a lot of jazz. The real usefulness of applications like this will only be apparent once huge databases of content can be tapped into, and more precise and smart matches to "deeper" catalog can be made. Just wait until someone finally gets around to hiring a thousand music college students to index deep metadata for ten million songs, and connect the dots in the music databases! The most successful services of the future will certainly combine deep profiling techniques with "musical DNA"–type approaches that try to scientifically chart the makings of any given track so that it can be compared to others.

In terms of reading about new music, Web sites like Metacritic. com, Acclaimedmusic.net, Allmusic.com, Mymixedtapes.com, and Muze.com provide resources and recommendations that help people find new music, but not one of them has quite become the *Reader's Digest* of online music, yet. Look for that void to be filled. The combination of strong editorial resources with innovative software technology will produce some very lucrative services in the future.

Collaborative filtering software holds strong potential for the music business. This technology is designed to help consumers find products that they might like, based on the buying and preference habits of other people who have similar habits. This approach sounds logical but has turned out to be less than trivial to actually deploy; witness the confusion that Amazon users experience when the bookseller's software keeps on recommending the latest Winnie the Pooh videos just because you have ordered a few for the kids, three years ago. This rather crude version of collaborative filtering for music fans is already commonplace at Amazon.com, providing recommendations in the form of, "Customers who bought John Mayer and James Taylor also bought Michael Franks and Dave Matthews."

Since the success and popularity of MIT's Firefly, countless other collaborative filtering and recommendation systems have emerged. Many of these ventures were too early for the market and could not be sustained without a strong flow of revenues. The second coming of enterprises in this turf should be quite exciting, though.

One such enterprise is Musicmatch. The Musicmatch system combines editorial expertise with community-based patterns of listening behavior and guides users through artist-based channels to find new music. This feature could prove to be one of the keys to the success of online digital music distribution services. Says Mike McGuire, research director for media at GartnerG2 consulting, "Once you get beyond the transaction to that place where it's kind of magic, I think what you're doing is ensuring future transactions."

The smart money is going to be invested in finding ways to connect people to music.

Music Recognition

Music recognition software applications are on the rise, and include Shazam, Musikube, MusicPhone, and Mediaguide/YesNetworks. London's Shazam was an early entrant into this arena. The application is designed to give listeners more information about songs they are listening to, via mobile networks. When listening to a song on the radio, for example, all you have to do is dial a certain number and hold the cell phone up to the music source for 15 seconds. The software analyzes the sound clip against its continuously growing song database, and returns, via a link or in a text message format, the song title, artist, album, where to buy the ring tone or track, or the option to send a 30-second clip of the track to a friend. Shazam has more than one million users across Europe and Asia and has already generated sales of over three million tracks in the U.K. alone. The service, called MusicID, is now available in the U.S. via AT&T wireless (dial #43) and Virgin Mobile.

Within five years, most of the world's formally recorded music catalog is likely to be recognizable by software, whether it uses waveform analysis, audio spectrum comparisons, fingerprinting, or watermarking ID processes. This will forever change many other pieces of the puzzle, such as playlisting and sharing music, broadcast monitoring, and accounting for synchronization and public broadcasting. Once a given track can be identified, any large enough network of monitoring devices can track its public use and the creator of that track can, in theory, be appropriately remunerated. This touches the core of what performance rights organizations are all about: monitoring the use of music, and remunerating the rights holders. Will the PRO of the future be simply a software company that adds a few other values here and there, or will we have a global collection network that feeds the data to local societies? Accountants take note.

Digital A&R Empowerment

Digital technologies and software are also changing the way that the industry discovers new artists and hits, in a more subtle, work-flow-enhancing kind of way. Ultimately, having "ears" like Clive Davis, Ahmet Ertegun, or Phil Spector has little to do with technology, but for the A&R person, technology has become an indispensable tool. Quickly check out a band's Web site, listen to samples, "Google" artists and their track records, communicate via e-mail or instant messaging, and transfer files back and forth. What's more, the new monitoring technologies such as Mediabase now make it feasible for an A&R manager to get up-to-the-minute feedback from individual markets, both in terms of radio airplay as well as in terms of sales or PR coverage.

Many other developments are happening in this arena, some more unusual than others, and some utterly far-fetched. Remember the creativity of the digital kids. There is software that is designed to pick hit songs before they actually become hit songs, by using a combination of demographic data, previous hit song meta-information, local variants, and general statistical logic. In principle, the idea is to predict the likelihood that a song will become a hit, and to thus spend more or fewer market dollars on the release. Defraying the risk of a major new release, maybe? Similar things have been tried by Sonicbids (www.sonicbids.com) in the live concert sector, and to a certain degree by services such as Garageband.com—examples of reducing the risk and lowering the initial investment required to find out if something is worth the investment or not. Knowledge is leverage, right?

Pick-a-hit software collects data from songs, focusing on musical patterns such as melody, harmony, beat, tempo, rhythm, pitch, chord progression, and fullness of sound. It takes samples from previous hits, in order to detect similarities among extremely popular songs. Hit-picking software is rumored to have predicted the success of eight-time Grammy winner Norah Jones before she was widely known. The real promise in our view comes from the blending of traditional A&R hit picking with consumer research and discovery methods to create a better, more efficient system.

Upgradeable Music: Try-and-Buy Models

Some smart people in the music industry are going to take a hard look at the tactics already employed by video game developers, software manufacturers, and film producers and distributors. These companies will create products that are upgradeable and/or "windowed," and in so doing, will develop an ever-expanding array of formats and release schedules on which to sell music. What could this mean for music?

Recorded music has long been seen as a static product; once you buy it, it will remain the same. Today, technology makes it possible to not only sell that one product with twelve tracks on it, but also "up-sell" and "cross-sell" the buyer to related products such as more music, DVDs, fan clubs, tickets, and videos. This underlines our prediction that music revenues from the actual "content" sales will amount only to, say, a third of the total revenues. The rest will be achieved via the sale of related products and services.

In the software world, the thirty-day-free-trial idea has been very successful, allowing an interested user to try a product or service for thirty days at no charge, sometimes with slightly reduced or restricted features. They can then decide if they like it enough to pay for it, or stop using it. We see a similar path for music marketing in the future—and it will certainly be easier to implement with a digital product than with a physical product. After all, with the exception of their record clubs, the music industry giants didn't even know the names of their customers until the computer came along. Hundreds of millions of CDs were sold without either the record company or the retailer collecting any meaningful data. Today, any and all indications of interest in the work of an artist can be tracked and linked to a database of actual users and consumers. Music marketing can become an entirely different ball game. Digital technologies give us the power to reach hundreds of thousands of individuals, with individually designed messages—and up-selling, cross-selling, and reselling has become a lot more feasible.

Operating similarly to a shareware provider, an artist's marketing manager may offer a few preview tracks of a new act to some people who have indicated interest in them, or even offer the first few tracks or the entire album for free, in order for the new act to gain exposure. A television appearance may be tied to a download promotion or a premium SMS game. A lot of the battle will be to cut through the din of all the new stuff that's out there and get noticed.

Some artists or their managers may even go as far as paying people to download and provide quick feedback on the music, since ultimately the name of the digital content game will always be to get exposure, be discovered, and *then* monetize the fan base. This is the key issue that still seems to be out of reach for most major-label strategists: digital technologies will move the toll-gate down the road, not up—the consumers are ready to pay *if* they can be fully convinced that this is what they want.

Integrated Music Experiences

Performers and their managers are beginning to use technology to create new live forms of entertainment, and new delivery mechanisms that go directly to their fans. Imagine a concert where the audience can influence the selection of the songs performed by the band, by sending SMS messages to the band's stage manager, in real time. Imagine electronic ordering features that allow concert participants to order a copy of live performance from that show, via their cell phones or PDAs, right there and then.

Imagine a virtual concert that was streamed directly to subscribers, in a pay-per-view model, with the band playing on a studio soundstage, and the performance streaming live via satellite, and then subsequently made available as a digital archive to the subscriber base. As we have discussed, many bands are doing this already.

The Grateful Dead gave away all of their shows to their fans, *for free*, allowing them to tape and exchange live concerts. New services such as DiscLive, eMusic, Livephish.com, and Rockslide are heading in the same direction. Add new wireless technologies such as WiFi, WiMAX, and Bluetooth to the mix, and artists could, in theory, play live concerts while distributing their music directly to fans at the show in real time, or after the show. The possibilities are endless.

Likely, these ideas will be utterly far-fetched for some artists, and a possibly crucial component for others—technology's ambivalent blessings and curses.

Megatrends that Will Impact the Future of Music

The music business, at roughly $75 billion in global revenues, including concerts, merchandising, CD sales, and publishing, is still relatively small compared to many other industries. Of the global entertainment economy of over $1.1 trillion, it makes up less than 10 percent.

As with most highly volatile businesses, many trends that are impacting business, culture, and society at large are impacting the music business even more directly, due to the intangible nature of its products and services. What can be more transient than a song, a memory that comes back with a tune you heard a long time ago, or the feeling you had when you last heard a particular singer? Trends in how people live, work, and interact are of great importance to the music business, and knowing how to recognize a trend often leads to recognizing a specific opportunity that may result from it—and opportunity recognition ultimately fuels the entrepreneurial fires, and it is different across the cultural landscape.

Let us now examine some of these trends and see what consequences they may have on the future of music. If you are really into music, understanding these trends may lead you to uncover some great opportunities.

The Accelerating Pace and Scope of Diversity

While in the days before digital networks, a major problem was a considerable lack of true diversity, choice, and variety, tomorrow's problem will be the reverse. Technology will give us more and more unfettered, low-cost, all-you-can-eat access—more television channels, hundreds of millions of Web pages, digital news feeds, SMS alerts, e-books, streaming media, digital photography, and so on. To be sure, having more options does not automatically mean having more diversity, but if we look at what is happening in the U.S. or in Western Europe, one can hardly label the existing "content" offerings as being devoid of diversity.

In Europe, diversity in television is palpable; in most European countries, one can watch television programs in four or five languages. Public broadcasters do a fairly good job of offering general-interest television programs that don't have to be advertising supported, and "alternative" stations such as ARTE show art films and independent fare. In the end, digital television can only truly take off if diversity is the guiding principle.

Another big factor in the growth of diversity is that, in the future, media will become less and less "push" and more and more "pull," with the typical couch potato turning into a "couch program director," a spontaneous "couch producer," or a even a "couch publisher." That is because most consumers like the feeling of choice and control that "pull" offerings afford. This is one of the reasons that heavy Internet users watch so much less television. Imagine what would happen if all television programs were also available on the various digital networks, as well, and if the PC and television were a single device—and that is indeed starting to happen with the idea of "entertainment center" PCs. Note that the couch will remain, either way, as digital technologies move from the office and the workspace to the living rooms and bedrooms.

With the advent of true diversity and multiplicity emerge issues of overstimulation and information overload, and the puzzling challenges of how people will deal with this vast surplus of information and media. This, in our view, is a very serious issue that far outweighs the concerns of digital piracy and economic changes caused by digital distribution. Let's take a look at why and how technology creates diversity, in general, and why it will do the same in the music business.

Today, movie theaters largely still employ the traditional courier-powered delivery of films, and, using fairly cheap but high-resolution analog projectors, project them onto the silver screen. Most of the innovation in the past has not come from upgrades in the projection equipment but from much improved sound systems, and also not from any improvements in standard business practice. The main reason that 95 percent of the films that are being released do not even make it into the cinemas is that it is just too expensive for a theater owner to order a copy of the reel, put it on the program, and have very few people show up.

And why would only a few people show up? Is this movie really a stinker? Are the actors doing a lousy job, was the script bad, or was it not worth seeing? That may be the case in *some* instances, but the real reason is that niche-market films rarely make it in the system of top-down media. It's simply too expensive to distribute physical copies of the reels to the thousands of places that could find audiences for lesser-known productions. It is mostly in allegedly hip and "buzzy" places, such as Soho, Cambridge, Berkeley, Amsterdam, and Barcelona, that we find cinemas that cater to a crowd that appreciates something different than the sex, violence, and special effects that Hollywood seems bent on feeding us. Sound familiar? It is the same reason that we don't tend to hear music that only twenty-five thousand people around the globe will enjoy. Even if these people would really, deeply enjoy the music, the present physical distribution system cannot easily support it, and there is no big profit in it. Economic rules and the quest for profit throttle diversity. If this hurdle can be removed—if digital technologies allow the seamless dissemination of media to any destination, any time, at a marginal cost—then we will see more diversity in what people want to see or hear. Technological progress begets choice, which begets diversity.

With the advent of digital technology, it is now theoretically feasible to distribute every single motion picture in existence to every single theater, for a fraction of the cost. This is good news for people who like diversity, and we believe that in the end, everyone does. Flawless digital copies of films can be delivered via satellite, DVD, or otherwise, and once digital projectors are installed in more locations, even a cinema with only thirty seats can do well on a mixed fare of eclectic screenings. Think Paris in the 1980s, or the student-union film clubs that many colleges in America offer today.

Most theater owners are reluctant to shell out the cash for these new technologies, but eventually, the equipment will become much cheaper. Before we know it, it'll be next door. A Lightning 6000 DLP projector, which still does not project as well as an analog projector running film, costs a whopping $75,000. But watch these prices melt very quickly while the quality gains in leaps and bounds. Ultimately, chances are that there will be numerous small theaters with digital systems and low prices, while a lot of large theaters will still project from the reels, as well.

But, you ask, what makes us think that anyone will want to see a movie from a hot new director from Poland, rather than see Spielberg's latest epic? Our answer: diversity is inspiring, and people *do* open up to it when it's readily available. Inspiration, ultimately, is important to everyone. Just like food, the results of simply offering many options are astounding. McDonald's is in every single town in America and in most cities in Europe, yet not everyone eats at McDonald's all the time. There are so many options, and a Big Mac is just one of them. Germans now have Chinese food, Italians serve sushi, and London serves any kind of food you can possibly think of. Those are welcome changes, compared to only twenty years ago. Diversity is also exponential because it breeds awareness, which in turn breeds more desire for diversity.

Will people continue to buy the mass-market music products that they buy today, if all these other options were instantly, easily, and cheaply available? Would they stay connected to the "push pipeline," or would they start to exert their "pull?" Well, some will and some won't, but the bottom line is that diversity ultimately creates a larger and more balanced market. Diversity marks the end of any monopoly. We have a true "music monopoly" today, and it is putting a serious damper on really growing the business.

Of course, the incumbent masters of push will do everything they can to prevent the business from changing beyond their control, be it in film, music, television, radio, or books. This is what Scott Dinsdale, Executive Vice President at the Motion Picture Association of America (MPAA), said at the Digital Media Summit in early 2003, according to Wired News (www.wired.com). When asked to summarize Hollywood's attitude toward the PC and the computer industry, he said, "You don't screw with me, I won't screw with you. Don't play a movie on a PC ever again, and I won't say a word."

The refusal of the record labels and publishing companies to make their music available for licensing under a flexible or flat-fee basis restricts the true power of diversity from being harnessed. We believe that these licensing issues will eventually be resolved, most likely by legislative—i.e., non-voluntary—means, and we may see levies and compulsory flat-fee arrangements abound. Access and distribution will no longer be the issue, but selection and discovery will be.

Without a doubt, technological advances have always led to a higher degree of diversity, and the music business will be no exception. Cars have led to wider travel patterns, cheap air travel has led to a wide variety of vacation options, cable television has led to a vast increase of available programs, and the Internet has led to a wide variety of sources of news being available to just about anyone. To be sure, not all of this was always to the advantage, or even the liking, of all involved participants—witness the disgruntled locals of Southern Spain having to deal with EasyJet discharging hundreds of bargain-hunting punters from Manchester every few hours. It all comes out in the wash, though . . .

During the times of "music as a product," mass-market albums marketed with million-dollar watering cans reigned supreme, and diversity was relegated to niche markets that were often struggling to stay solvent. In the future of music, the aggregate power of niche markets will exceed the importance of mass markets, and diversity will be the default setting.

The Changing Paradigms of Work and Leisure

The social theorist and oft-quoted guru Abraham Maslow pointed out a very significant trend in modern society: as we move from the Information Society to the "Dream Society"—a society in which emotions, stories, experiences, and intangible values vastly gain in importance—the hitherto all-important basic needs such as food, clothes, and shelter will become less important; they will be a given. Increasingly, it will become important to strive for self-realization and personal satisfaction, however it is defined. Maslow's hierarchy of needs aptly describes the trends towards the increased impor-tance of social interaction, acknowledgment, and self-realization, as opposed to physical needs and security.

This trend, and of course the global economic realities that now pretty much dictate life-long learning and extreme professional flex-ibility, will have significant impact on the definition of "work." These realities will then create more need and room for the enjoyment of media, and will also result in creating a surge of interest in careers that deal with emotions and experiences, such as art, writing, story-telling, filmmaking, dance, acting, composition, and performance of all kinds. In short, our society is likely to drastically expand its horizons with a growing emphasis on knowledge, arts, experiences, and emotions, and "caring" jobs such as health and therapy—all of which will impact the economic realities of people who work in the music industry.

This development, in tandem with the tremendous power that modern audio production, distribution, and broadcasting technologies give to just about everyone, will mean that there will be strong trends towards creating your own music, whether it is cut-and-paste, or actually "hand-made." And, there will be emphasis on being part of a global music community, rather than simply being a music consumer. One can, of course, argue that mountains of "musical landfill" may be created by the hordes of amateurs who will be set free to create in the digital landscape. That may happen, but still, it cannot really be wrong to give some means of self-expression to a larger number of people, provided that potent filtering and selection methodologies exist to help the cream rise to the top.

Another important aspect of these Maslowian transformations of priorities is that it is very likely that people will constantly shift between different jobs or other economically motivated activities, and will maintain more than one moneymaking occupation at any given time. Thus, they will continue to learn and attain new qualifications all the time. In fact, some people may even be paid to not work in the traditional sense—perhaps via an increase in grants and fellowships—so that society at large can benefit from their "carefree" contributions to the whole. This is a potential new role for visionaries, inventors, entrepreneurs, and artists.

This free-flowing approach to work and ultimately to money, as well, may seem outright scary to many, until it becomes commonly accepted that the value of people is in our ability to experience unique interplays of brain, heart, and body. This will also have great impact on the music business: more time to participate and contribute, more desire to do so, and more room, time, and means to consume music. In fact, "consumption" and "contribution" may eventually be mixed in so many ways that they ultimately become indistinguishable. Either way, music and all art will have a growing role in our society, much bigger than we have ever seen, and related business activities will profit exponentially.

To partake in these opportunities, we must try to deeply understand what people want. We must also understand where, how, and at what time they want it, and then make matches with artists that fit the bill. Once we understand this, then the next big step is marketing—and the art of marketing will probably undergo the biggest changes in this entire puzzle.

The Unobtrusive Expansion of Technology

Technology is no longer a big deal in its own right—very few people still marvel at things that simply work like they're supposed to, such as airplanes or cell phones. Sophisticated and almost-always-on communication has become a default mindset for many of us. Just as the telephone and the car have been seamlessly integrated into our lives, so will digital media technology be woven into every part of our daily routines. It will simply be a part of our lifestyle. Today, the computer sits in the office and the television sits in the living room, but with media entertainment centers, streaming media servers, TIVO, Web TV, and the Nokia Visual Radio, the borders are already starting to blur. Cell phones already have a lot more computing power than the first Altair computers did, way back in 1975. Cell phones are quickly turning into omnipotent mobile computing devices that take pictures, play music, stream videos, manage contact data and calendars, surf the Web, connect us with others, and direct us to the nearest ATM. Talking about unobtrusive—imagine your wrist-watch having these capabilities.

Our reliance on technology is increasing every day, for better or for worse. We rely on cars, trains, and airplanes for transportation, satellites, cable, and wireless for communication, computers and storage devices to keep our data, television and the Internet for information, Global Positioning Systems to find our way, online banking and online trading for our money, and on and on. The mind-boggling pace of invention is ever increasing and the technological imperative ("what can be done must be done") all too often reigns supreme until some human sensibility takes over again. While the Agricultural Society lasted ten thousand years and the Industrial Society lasted two hundred years, we sometimes wonder how long the Information Society will last before it gives birth to something even less tangible— what the Danish Future Institute calls the Dream Society, but what we will simply call the "Experience Economy." All of this is good news to the future of music: the more the Experience Economy takes root, the more value will be placed on music.

It is perhaps even more impressive to note how, finally, technology is actually adapting to people, rather than the reverse. In the '70s, '80s, and even the '90s, many technologies required that unwitting users make some serious changes in their habits and adapt to the hard-wired logic of the machine. Great examples of this are online reservation systems such as Sabre, or the first wireless devices, and last but not least, the Windows operating system.

Today, however, no technological innovation really succeeds unless it is perfectly in synch with what people will accept. The bar has been raised, the consumer can see behind the curtain, and comparisons have become easy. In the future, preventing customers from doing things that they have grown used to will equal a quickly executed death blow.

For the music business, this means that any innovation that will be offered to the marketplace must be without any catches. It must be flat-out in synch with what the consumer will accept and wants, and its integration into the daily lives of the average music consumer must be unobtrusive and effortless. In other words: keep it simple, and give the customers what they want.

The Overload of Information and Media

On the flip side of this tidal wave of cool technology, we are facing a unique situation. We have morphed from the politically motivated self-constraints of corporate media in the U.S., and the sluggishness of public broadcasting in Europe, to a violent blast of media and information coming at us 24/7/365. Cell phones and other wireless devices are shaping up to be a major force in information distribution, and like it or not, there will be no escape. We will all have to learn how to deal with a fifteen-mile-long virtual buffet of media and data.

EMarketer (www.emarketer.com) predicts that digital television will be at a 70-percent penetration level in U.S. households by 2007, and within ten years after that, a pretty much unlimited number of television and digital radio channels will be available to almost everyone in the "connected world." Imagine one thousand-plus digital programs to choose from, in addition to what is freely available on the Internet, where the amount of available information doubles every eighteen months. This may almost make you wish you weren't connected!

Digital radio will undergo similar development, with digital radio receivers (XM and Sirius) for cars already in the U.S.. Comcast and other digital cable providers have launched movie-on-demand services, and online gaming is gaining tens of thousands of users per month, with one of the most popular games, Sims Online by Electronic Arts, already ensnaring over three hundred thousand fiercely loyal subscribers every month—that's *paid* subscribers.

And this is in addition to the good old killer app of the 'Net, e-mail, which is still on the rise everywhere, and which is still the top-rated item on the to-do list for people who use the Internet. Research shows that in some countries, business people spend two hours per day just dealing with their e-mail. Add SMS, chats, instant messaging, news, and networking to this picture, then consider the fact that the day still only has twenty-four hours. It looks like a serious time crunch, all around.

Let us revisit the documented trend, once again: heavy Internet users spend 38 percent less time watching television. What does this mean for the convergence of the television and the computer, and for advertising? If and when television programs (and commercials!) can be watched on the Internet, will these programs just be one of the gazillion channels that people have available to them? Also, interestingly, people are spending more money on "content" (media) all the time. A full 80 percent of the U.S. population has readily accepted monthly fees from $25 to $80 for cable television, despite how many said no one would ever pay for more television. They now are more willing to pay for content online, as well: in 2001, U.S. consumers spent $670 million on online content, and in 2002 that figure doubled to $1.3 billion (eMarketer), despite the serious economic turmoil that engulfed us at that time.

According to research by the Pew Internet group, one of the most common inhibitors for people to use the Internet is the concern of being overwhelmed with stuff, and being deluged with information, right along with concerns of maintaining privacy. And this is still early in the game! At the same time, a 2002 eMarketer survey showed that 33 percent of kids between 8 and 17 years old would choose the Internet over television, radio, and the telephone, if they could have only one of them. Clearly, today's kids and the next generations to come will grow up taking the Internet for granted (like electricity or water), and will be accustomed to filtering through the flood of information that pours through it. Contrast this with the old, pre-'Net days when we had to buy seven newspapers to get enough objective information on any given subject. Life has changed profoundly.

Just imagine yourself having access to a ten-thousand-plus song collection anytime, together with streams of news and sports events, SMS messages, e-mail, chats, and instant messages, and your favorite games—all in a device the size of your wallet. How do you decide what to do? Do you become an information junkie, constantly checking your e-mails while sitting in a conference, sending text messages while standing at a red light, talking to your colleagues using VoIP while watching a news stream from CNN? How do you decide what to do when? Which news to watch, which music to hear, which mails to read, and which to ignore? Will the "technical imperative" drive us ballistic, and trigger a perpetual information overload in our head? Will you feel "left out" when you're not constantly barraged by information and media? Will this lead to an utterly cluttered society, with mountains of homegrown and half-baked content plugging up the pipelines—and our brains?

This issue will be one of the major focus areas for companies concerned with digital media commerce. In fact, ultimately the question of *what you pay attention to* will completely replace the question of how you get access to it. It's all about exposure and discovery.

The Surveillance Society and Concerns of Privacy

One of the prime concerns that people have these days is that everything they do is somehow logged, archived, and monitored—just a few steps shy of *The Truman Show*, the movie in which an insurance salesman discovers that his life is actually a television show. With ever-new ways of allegedly promoting national security, the U.S. government keeps coming up with new surveillance schemes every other week, and the recording industry lobby is not far behind when, under the cloak of anti-piracy, it tracks the file-sharing activities of millions of online music fans.

To prove the point, in late 2001, the RIAA unsuccessfully tried to piggy-back their stringent anti-file-sharing proposals, which would have made it legal to invade people's computers to search for illegal

MP3 files or to sabotage their systems if they did, onto a national security bill that was launched in response to the September 11 terrorist attacks. George Orwell couldn't have written a better plot.

The surveillance society has manifested itself in the millions of video cameras that are now in operation at public buildings, banks, intersection, gas stations, train stations, airports, and hospitals. It is also evident in the advent of machine-readable IDs and biometric security solutions. There exist today several initiatives that would, by design or by abuse, allow companies to track your every move on the Internet and other digital networks. One of these is the Microsoft.Net initiative. Together with credit card accounting and your phone bill, this flow of data can be used to create a watertight profile of you, and in the hands of the wrong people, can give rise to scary scenarios of misuse, such as screening people for employment by looking at their spending and traveling profiles, or determining people's political inclinations by looking at their media subscriptions, travel details, and online buying patterns.

Rightly, people are especially concerned about their privacy on the digital highway, where everything from book purchases to news-letter subscriptions to file downloading and DVD ordering can be tracked. A solution must be found if digital media is to be delivered to a large percentage of the population through the Internet and other digital networks, and stringent security measures and real privacy guarantees must be put into place—another good opportunity for enterprising startups.

Heart over Brain

The Information Society has up-ended the Industrial Society, and a new Experience Economy is hijacking the Information Society. The "first" Internet boom was partly fueled by the belief that by smartly sucking up infinite amounts of information and by ever-expanding our capacities for data-intake and knowledge, we could win the game, whatever it may be. In so doing, we could thus avoid being sucked into black holes, at least in commercial terms. In many ways, this thought process really reflected a belief in the illusion of the brain as the ultimate force behind self-expression and self-fulfillment. That is, "If I can learn and understand this, I could really *rule.*"

In good time, however, this self-inflation and these skillful self-deception schemes came back to bite us in the rear. Now, the bubble is burst—in fact, it burst years ago—and futurists are taking a good look at what exactly makes human knowledge and human intelligence unique, and certainly this will be reflected in the future of music. It seems obvious, of course, that human intelligence is not simply about the brain's ability to take in a lot of data points and to remember (and combine) them. Rather, it is the brain's ability to process the *actual, multidimensional experience* that makes the wheels of human intelligence go 'round.

The Copenhagen Institute for Future Studies, one of the leading futurist institutions in Europe and a great resource for ideas, has outlined the following factors that *the heart* has to offer (as opposed to the brain): experience, identity, aesthetics, esteem, impulse, and emotions—to which we would like to humbly add, intuition and foresight.

A high level of information and knowledge (i.e., "brain power") is often considered a default starting point in most professional situations these days, but now we are beginning to see an increasing emphasis on the somewhat ephemeral "soft skills." Ultimately, this emerging trend aligns neatly with the observation that technology now offers so many ways to get information and to fill up our know-how pools, that pure information is no longer a distinguishing factor in and of itself.

Far more importantly, plain information must make a connection to the subliminal—to the heart or . . . the spirit . . . if it is to emerge as a meaningful contribution. That is, the Internet has to offer us more than just information; we also need *experience*. This is mirrored in advertising and branding campaigns, where advertisers maximize the selling power of "the heart" by delivering emotional content, rather than purveying on-the-surface facts and objective data. After all, that is what sells a brand—the *perception* in the mind of the buyer—the feeling. This comes as no surprise to most music professionals. Music does not sell because of objective facts—e.g., "He is the fastest guitar player on earth"—but rather because it makes some miraculous connection to the heart. Music sells because it touches people.

And of course, let's also not forget the role of "the body" alongside the brain and the heart, since making music is always an expression of some body movement, and the body very strongly responds to music. The body is the vehicle for our expression, and as a result, is the manifestation of both the heart and the brain. Innovators in bodywork, such as the renowned Moshe Feldenkrais, have done a great deal of research into how awareness and "attitude" changes the bodily reactions to stimuli. They also have shown how much the body is governed by internal processes and mental images. When people are touched by music, it often results in real bodily sensations, in "real" and tangible experiences that are way beyond the logic of simply processing information.

We are moving towards a society in which the brain will certainly be quite busy, but the body will constantly be cared for and nurtured, and the heart will deliver the real value. And ubiquitous music will be our soundtrack.

Onto the Future

Futurist Alan Kay once said, "The best way to predict the future is to invent it." As we have seen in this book, there is a tremendous number of bright individuals hard at work developing new ways to create, deliver, market, and enjoy music. They are inventing the future of music. The "music like water" scenario is taking shape right before our eyes, as digital and wireless networks and consumer electronics mesh and wrap their orbits around the digital delivery of music. To be sure, the music business of today is vastly different than it was just a mere ten years ago, and the next ten years will be equally, if not more, transformative.

We hope that we have helped to invent a small part of the future of music by turning you on to some of the possible scenarios. Our goal is to kindle your imagination, provoke exploration, make you wonder about the possibilities, and egg you on to be a part of creating the future of music yourself. The simple truth of the matter is that music belongs to the people, not to the multinational corporations that have controlled and exploited it over the past seventy-five years or so. The people, both fans and musicians alike, will decide what kind of future we want. Rest assured that it will be very different from the past.

To be sure, it is impossible to predict the future of music with 100-percent accuracy. We are fully aware that many sections of this book will quickly be overtaken by real-time developments in the industry, and we could unquestionably publish a new chapter each month. Our work with the Future of Music is an ongoing process that we plan to continue to track and describe in subsequent revisions to this book, in our blog, and in our other, related projects.

We encourage anyone who has found this book to be interesting and informative to join us in a dynamic and interactive forum online at the Future of Music Web site (www.futureofmusicbook.com), where we plan to post downloadable updates to the book. The site also features our blog, a game, Web links, and live chats with the authors and with entrepreneurs, artists, and music business professionals from around the globe. We look forward to hearing from you.

This book is a required text for a course taught at Berklee College of Music, titled "The Future of Music and the Music Business." This course is taught online via Berklee's online extension school, Berkleemusic (www.berkleemusic.com). The online course is a place to learn about and explore the future of music from the point of view of artists, musicians, and businesspeople who are seeking to stay engaged in the music industry as it evolves. If you are interested in delving deeper into the subject and connecting with others actively engaged in a music career, we encourage you to take the online course.

Both of us provide strategic consulting and business advisory services to companies and individuals in the music and entertainment industries. You can contact us via the futureofmusicbook.com Web site for more information. We hope that your future is bright and musical.

Index

About the Authors

PHOTO BY CRAIG REED

Dave Kusek is a musician who has been inventing the future of music for the past twenty-five years. He was one of the first to capitalize on the commercial potential of computers and music. As an early synthesizer and electronic music pioneer, Dave cut his teeth on innovation. At the age of nineteen, he co-invented electronic drums at Synare, which helped ignite the disco era. In 1980, he founded the first music software company, Passport Designs, which made it possible for musicians to record and produce their music at home with its award-winning software.

Kusek is also a co-developer of the Musical Instrument Digital Interface (MIDI) standard that opened up electronic music to literally millions of people. His efforts, along with others, set the stage for the desktop music market that we have today. In 1993, Kusek, with A&M Records, designed and developed the first commercially available enhanced CD that connected audio CDs to a personal computer. He also produces interactive DVDs for BMG Music, Windham Hill Records, and Berklee Press.

Today, Dave Kusek innovates at Berklee College of Music in Boston, Mass., the premier school for aspiring professional musicians for over half a century. Dave is Vice President of Berklee Media, the continuing education division of the college. In that capacity, Dave oversees some of the college's most visionary projects. These include: the college's online extension school Berkleemusic (www.berkleemusic.com), a major initiative to expand music education worldwide; Berklee Shares (www.berkleeshares.com), a venture that taps the potential of digital networks and music content licensing by making a broad selection of Berklee's curriculum free and universally available online; and, Berklee Press (www.berkleepress.com) the publishing arm of the college. An Associate Professor of Music Business at Berklee, Kusek also provides strategic consulting and advisory services to companies and individuals involved in the music and entertainment industries.

Kusek has been quoted in *Billboard, Boston Globe, New York Times, Wired, Christian Science Monitor, Associated Press,* and *San Francisco Chronicle.* He has been a speaker and lecturer at Berklee College of Music, MacWorld, Comdex, PC World, NAMM, AES, and California State University.

Dave lives near Boston and can be contacted at dkusek@digitalcowboys.com.

Gerd Leonhard is a respected music futurist and oft-quoted visionary, a well-known music industry executive and music business entrepreneur, a sought-after strategic adviser and music industry super-node—and still a performer (guitar), writer, and producer. A native of Germany, Gerd has spent more than twenty years in the U.S. music, e-commerce, and entertainment technology industries, and is equally at home in the U.S. as well as in Europe. He currently resides in Basel, Switzerland.

During the dot.com days, Gerd was the founder and President/ CEO of LicenseMusic.com, a company that revolutionized music licensing, reducing the average transaction time for music licenses from six weeks to two hours. LicenseMusic, Inc. served thousands of clients from 1996–2002, including Disney, Paramount Pictures, and Fox TV.

He is the Founder and CEO of ThinkAndLink (TAL), a boutique advisory agency based in Basel, Switzerland and San Francisco. TAL connects people, ideas, companies, and resources in the converging sectors of entertainment and technology, and catalyzes their development. As CEO of ThinkAndLink, he serves as Senior Advisor to Media Rights Technologies, BlueBeat, and ShareTheMusic Networks. Gerd sits on the Advisory Board of Musicrypt, Inc., and works with dozens of startups and new ventures in the entertainment and technology industries in Europe and the U.S.

Gerd served as the Executive Producer of the pan-European talent event EuroPopDays, as Expert Advisor on the Cultural Industries to the European Commission in Brussels in 1993–1996, and as Senior Strategic Adviser to Rightscom Ltd. (London).

Gerd graduated with a diploma in Jazz Performance (Guitar) from Boston's Berklee College of Music (1987), and won the college's highly acclaimed Quincy Jones Jazz Masters Award. His performance credits include touring internationally, including opening engagements for major acts such as Miles Davis.

He has been quoted in *Billboard*, *Variety*, *Hollywood Reporter*, *San Francisco Chronicle*, *Business2.0*, *Wall Street Journal*, and *Wired*, and continues to speak, moderate, and/or present at the music industry's biggest events. He publishes his music business visions at MusicFuturist (www.musicfuturist.com), and is the founder of the MusicEntrepreneurs Network (www.musicentrepreneurs.com), a network platform for entrepreneurs in the music business. Visit his Web site at www.gerdleonhard.com, and check out his blog at gerdleonhard.typepad.com.

Reviews of *The Future of Music*

A solid look at how the music industry is healthy even if the music business is not. One of the best takes today on what a "pool of music" could mean to the artists, record labels and consumers.—The Register

I think your book is the best music business book I have ever read! I have recommended it at our recent meetings.—Franklin Spicer, Los Angeles Songwriter Co-op

Comments from *futureofmusicbook.com:*

The Future of Music *is a prophetic book that nails right down where it's at. It's a must to read for everyone in Internet, media and music industries.*—John Mark

I just started reading your book and I can't put it down!—Sue Frenz

I just finished The Future of Music. *Incredible read. I'm abuzz with inspiration and hope*—Chris Farrell

I have just purchased The Future of Music. *Quite an extraordinarly book, to say the least.*—Bob Beland

Great book. I have bought over a dozen copies for colleagues.—Richard Rees

We loved your book and our entire team has been given the assignment to read it. A resounding THANK YOU for raising the consciousness of our customers and audience. We will be recommending your book to everyone we know.—Amity Carriere, hotlocalmusic.com

Thank you for giving everyone a reason to believe in the wondrous vision of the future of music.—Joe Lefebvre

I just finished reading your book and I must say that I was floored. I was so impressed that someone had the guts to write a book about what the music business should be doing. Congratulations.—Dario Svidler